THE BLACK BOOK OF DAY TRADING

THE SPONSOR'S MANUAL FOR SURVIVING AND DOMINATING THE AUCTION

THE BLACK BOOK OF DAY TRADING

THE SPONSOR'S MANUAL FOR SURVIVING AND DOMINATING THE AUCTION

By - ANCIENT THE ARCHITECT

The Black Book of Day Trading: The Sponsor's Manual for Surviving and Dominating the Auction
© 2025 Ancient the Architect

Book cover © 2025 Ancient the Architect

Published by Health Is Luxury LLC
Hartford, Connecticut

ISBN 979-8-9922102-8-6

Printed in the United States of America

Disclaimer
This book is provided solely for educational purposes. Nothing herein should be interpreted as financial, legal, or investment advice. Day trading and derivatives trading carry significant risk, including the possible loss of all capital. Readers are solely responsible for their own trading decisions and should consult a qualified financial advisor before engaging in trading activity.

Table of Contents

Introduction — Read This Before You Begin
This is not a beginner's guide and it is not a motivational pep talk. It is an operating manual for day traders who want to stop donating liquidity and start operating with the same structural awareness as institutions. The introduction sets the frame: why this book exists, who it is for, and what standard will be demanded of you before you can survive in the auction.

- **CTA / Trend / Risk-Parity** – Vol-scaled grind or mechanical air pockets.

- **Corporate Executions (10b5-1 / Buybacks)** – Stealth absorption; support vanishes in blackout.

- **ETFs / Indexers / Rebalances** – Calendar gravity pins and jerks price.

- **HFT / Internalizers** – Microstructure monetizers; chop when sponsors are absent.

- **Discretionary Macro / Event** – Quiet load → one asymmetric strike.
  III. **The Venues & Pipes** – Lit, dark, internalized, and auction prints; order types that hide truth.
  IV. **Four Invisible Forces** – Benchmark pressure, dealer hedging regimes, liquidity vacuums, calendar gravity.
  V. **The Narrative Machine** – Stories decorate flows; ask who the headline enabled.
  VI. **Five Lies That Keep You Supplying Liquidity** – Levels as laws, volume as truth, etc.
  VII. **Case Files from the Command Room** – 10:17 Trap; Pin; 3:42 Squeeze; Vacuum Walk.
  VIII. **The Operator's Questions** – Urgency, clock, fuel, survivorship, and food chain.
  IX. **Four Modes of the Inner Room** – Surveillance, Probe, Campaign, Extraction & Reset.
  X. **The Operator's Oath** – Pin this above your screens.
  XI. **What Changes Starting Now** – From candle worship to sponsor alignment.

Position Before the Story, Exit Before the Crowd
Part 1: **Pre-Market Sponsor Recon** – Overnight futures, blocks, anomalies, sector tells → daily hypothesis.
Part 2: **Intraday Sponsor Confirmation** – Opening drive, VWAP behavior, profile shape, correlations.
Part 3: **Execution Translation** – Only A+ re-entry/defense moments, not chases.
Part 4: **The Two-Trade Discipline** – One to two pristine shots or stand down.
Mindset Shift – Align with the room that controls the narrative.

How the Market Hunts, Traps, and Transfers Capital
Part 1: **Liquidity Zones** – Highs/lows, round numbers, anchored VWAPs, nodes.
Part 2: **True Break Hunts vs. False Break Hunts** – Continuation vs. stop-run reversals.
Part 3: **Pre-Hunt Context Clues** – Compression, delta divergence, vacuums, correlation asymmetry.
Part 4: **Execution Traps** – Breakout, Flush, VWAP Flip, Gap Fill.
Part 5: **Spotting the Sponsor in Real Time** – Absorption, initiative drives, defensive reclaims.
Part 6: **Build the Morning Liquidity Map** – Routine marks and alerts.
Part 7: **The Exit Principle** – Get out before the story reaches the crowd.
Closing Mindset – Predator, not prey.

the parent phase.

Part 7: **Using the Cycle in Your Trading** – Bias-aligned intraday execution.

Closing Mindset – Trade the campaign, not isolated candles.

Why Gamma Is the X-Ray of Price

Part 1: **The Dealer's Job** – Delta hedging, long vs. short gamma regimes.

Part 2: **Pin Risk & Magnet Strikes** – OI gravity, especially into Fridays.

Part 3: **Intraday Gamma Behavior** – Compression vs. acceleration tells.

Part 4: **The Expiry Engine** – Monthly/quarterly resets and post-Opex volatility release.

Part 5: **Gamma Flip Zones** – Behavioral flips above call walls / below put walls.

Part 6: **Tactical Applications** – Map OI, set expectations, anchor to strikes, clock + VWAP overlays.

Part 7: **Case Files** – TSLA pin, SPY short-gamma cascade, AAPL unwind.

Part 8: **Operator's Gamma Checklist** – The five pre-session questions.

Closing Mandate – You're trading math, not mood.

Absolute Institutional Architecture + U.S. Equities Tactical Execution

Phase 1: **Overnight Positioning (Global Sweep)** – Inventory/sentiment shaping; pre-market tells.

Phase 2: **Pre-Market Recon** – 8:30 data shakes, VWAP

dislocations, first magnets.

Phase 3: **Open Sequence (Trap Deployment)** – False breaks, VWAP games, front-loaded volume.

Phase 4: **Midday Positioning (Quiet Kill)** – Passive absorption, VWAP anchoring.

Phase 5: **Power Hour (Hammer Drop)** – Closing control, risk transfer, tomorrow's trap.

Black Book Commandments – Phases, VWAP gravity, overnight staging, invisible midday, close as setup.

Chapter 8 — The Sponsor Archetypes Playbook...*pg 48*

Decoding the Forces Behind the Tape

- **Archetype 1: Long-Only Benchmark Fund** – VWAP/close urgency; fade exhaustion or pre-position.

- **Archetype 2: Dealer / Options MM** – Gamma regime dictates compression/violence; trade the hedge.

- **Archetype 3: CTA / Trend / Risk Parity** – Ride grind; exit fast on vol flip.

- **Archetype 4: Corporate Execution (Buybacks / 10b5-1)** – Quiet bid; beware blackout cliffs.

- **Archetype 5: ETF / Index Rebalancer** – Calendar magnets; violent closes.

- **Archetype 6: HFT / Internalizer** – Chop regime; size down or sit out.

- **Archetype 7: Discretionary Macro / Event** – Catalyst strike into vacuum.

- **Capital Deployment Pyramid** – Preservation / Operational / Aggression layers.

- **Risk per Trade** – 0.5–1.0% baseline; cut during drawdowns.

- **Scaling In/Out** – Pre-planned adds; peel at structural stations.

- **Drawdown Survival** – Cut size, stop hopping, narrow windows.

- **Aggressive Growth Windows** – Data-earned, temporary size expansion.

- **Institutional Risk Lens** – Trade / Portfolio / Strategic risk alignment.

- **Commandments** – Size follows data; aggression is earned.

Chapter 11 — The Flow Advantage...*pg 65*

Understanding Liquidity and Market Energy

- **Why Price Moves** – Removal, aggression, or absorption break.

- **Liquidity Pools & Kill Zones** – Above highs / below lows.

- **Energy Transfer** – Released → redirected.

- **Institutional Triggers** – Stop runs, gaps, absorption withdrawals.

- **Execution Edge** – Enter into the release, not after.

- **Build Your Liquidity Map** – Highs/lows, VWAP bands, strikes, nodes.

- **Psychological Edge** – From "attacked" to "orchestrated."

Chapter 12 — Precision Timing...*pg 69*

The Professional's Clock

- **Three Core Windows** – Opening Drive; Midday Drift; Power Close.

- **Event-Driven Windows** – CPI/NFP/FOMC, earnings, OpEx, Fed, geopolitics.

- **Clock Mindset** – Hunt when vol+liq converge; stand down otherwise.

- **Case Study: Timing Saves Capital** – Same pattern, opposite outcomes.

- **Build Time Discipline** – A+ windows, shutdown times, P/L by hour.

- **Psychological Edge** – Focus compression, FOMO control.

Chapter 13 — Capital Warfare: How Professionals Deploy and Protect Money

- **Capital as Ammunition** – Not a scoreboard, but finite weaponry.

- **Preservation as Offense** – Survive until the fat pitch arrives.

- **Risk Per Trade: Non-Negotiable** – Sizing backwards from risk, not greed.

- **Deployment Models** – Fixed risk; tiered conviction; pre-planned scaling.

- **The Kill Shot Mindset** – Probing shots vs. unleashing maximum size.

- **Capital Drain Awareness** – Bleed rate analysis; avoiding slow death in chop.

- **Cash as a Weapon** – Flat is holding your army for real battle.

- **Institutional Layer** – Desks measure drawdown tolerance, not "green days."

- **Action Protocol** – Daily/weekly limits, bleed tracking, scaling rules, kill-shot readiness.

4.   **Speed & Latency** – Hardware, network, platform stability as survival.

5.   **Tape & Flow Tools** – Time & sales, order book, volume profile, VWAP anchors, options flow.

6.   **Automation Without Abdication** – Algos as assistants, not commanders.

7.   **Building the Console** – Clarity, speed, stealth. **Operator's Commandments of Technology** – Every click a tax; every leak a tell; every lag sabotage.

Chapter 16 — The Professional Trader's Code: Non-Negotiables...*pg 89*

-      **Law 1 — Capital is Oxygen**

-      **Law 2 — One Career-Ending Mistake Is Always Lurking**

-      **Law 3 — The Market Owes You Nothing**

-      **Law 4 — Risk Small, Scale Big Only When Earned**

-      **Law 5 — Every Trade Expires When Its Reason Dies**

-      **Law 6 — Personal Life = Trading Life**

-      **Law 7 — Never Pay the Same Tuition Twice**

-      **Law 8 — The Trade Ends With the Plan**

-      **Law 9 — Your Ego Is the Counterparty**

- **Weapon 3: Context Lock** – Higher frame held against micro noise.

- **Weapon 4: Two-Tier Risk View** – Structural + psychological risk filters.

- **Weapon 5: Silent Countdown** – Override instinct with rationality.

- **Weapon 6: Posture Reset** – Physical repositioning resets mind.

- **Weapon 7: Mental Auto-Scaling** – Instant size cut on slippage.

- **Weapon 8: Detached Observation Mode** – Analyst state > emotional trader.

- **Weapon 9: End-of-Day Amnesia** – Reset slate; yesterday is irrelevant.

Chapter 19 — Failure Autopsy: Why 99% of Traders Die... *pg 105*

I. **The Anatomy of a Trading Death** – Stacked violations, compounding failure.
II. **Failure Mode #1: Over-Leverage** – The Widowmaker.
III. **Failure Mode #2: Tilt Loops** – The Afternoon Spiral.
IV. **Failure Mode #3: Phase Ignorance** – The Open Drive Victim.
V. **Failure Mode #4: Calendar Amnesia** – The Fed Victim.
VI. **Failure Mode #5: Narrative Addiction** – The Bagholder.
VII. **Failure Mode #6: Over-Trading** – The Scalper Corpse.
VIII. **Failure Mode #7: Ego Override** – The Blow-Up Hero.

IX. **Unified Cause of Death** – All corpses share the same root chain.

X. **The Autopsy Oath** – Survival commandments pinned to the screen.

Chapter 20 — The Tactical Day Structure of a Pro...*pg 112*

Segment 1 — Pre-Market War Room – Battlefield, playbook, triggers, guardrails.

Segment 2 — Opening Shockwave – Observation, control zones, early traps.

Segment 3 — Post-Open Trend Test – Confirmation or rejection of morning bias.

Segment 4 — Midday Grind – Capital-preservation mode.

Segment 5 — Power Hour Setup – Afternoon narrative and squeezes.

Segment 6 — Closing Drive – Order imbalances, discipline, post-mortem.

Why It Works – Energy matched to probability; tilt contained.

Chapter 21 — The Psychology of Capital Preservation...*pg 117*

- **The Capital Mindset Shift** – Account as ammo cache, not scoreboard.

- **Three Dimensions of Preservation** – Financial, Emotional, Reputational.

- **Core Rule of Survivorship** – Must be armed when the fat pitch comes.

- **The Preservation Protocol** – Ammo budget, offensive vs. defensive tags, energy tracking, kill switch, reputation audits.

- **Why Boredom Equals Survival** – Longevity > excitement.

Chapter 22 — The Execution Mind...*pg 122*

- **Why Execution Bottlenecks Edge** – Ideas mean nothing without precision.

- **Build the Execution Mind** – Pre-decisions, friction reduction, emotional firewall.

- **Instant Loss Acceptance** – Stops are contracts; no negotiation.

- **Exiting Aggressively When Wrong** – Tactical retreat > hope.

- **Maintaining the Human Edge** – Machine discipline + human adaptability.

- **Execution Flow of a Pro** – Morning → Live session → Post-trade notes.

Chapter 23 — The Longevity Blueprint...*pg 127*

1. **Reality of Cycles** – Hot streaks and cold patches are natural.

2. **Capital Preservation as Career Skill** – Floor rules and scaling discipline.

3. **The Energy Account** – Mental fuel tracked alongside capital.

4. **Continuous Edge Refinement** – Strategies decay; quarterly audits required.

5. **Avoiding Psychological Decay** – Complacency and blind spots.

6. **Building a Life Outside the Screen** – External arenas build resilience.

7. **Legacy Thinking** – Fund, teaching, capital beyond yourself.
   Bottom Line – Survival is a system, not luck.

Chapter 24 — The Closing Playbook: Survival, Growth, Domination...*pg 133*

1. **Survival Mode** – Laws of oxygen capital and tilt avoidance.

2. **Growth Mode** – Scale without sloppiness; data-driven capital allocation.

3. **Domination Mode** – Sponsor-level operation; engineering outcomes.

4. **Three-Mode Integration** – Shifting gears fluidly between survival, growth, domination.

5. **Self-Override Protocol** – Emergency brake against tilt.

6. **20-Year View** – Long-horizon discipline for true wealth.

7. **Closing Mandate** – Preparation is the floor you fall to.

1.   **The Truth About Why You're Failing** –
      Excuses stripped bare.

2.   **The Switch** – The moment you decide to operate
      like a sponsor.

3.   **The Long War** – Thinking in decades, not
      fireworks.

4.   **The Real Wealth** – Freedom > scoreboard.

5.   **The Trader's Oath** – Survival, execution,
      refinement, discipline.

6.   **Your New Baseline** – Precision, professionalism,
      iteration.
      Closing Call – There is no someday. There is
      only today.

Appendix A — Operator's Lexicon

The operational vocabulary of the command room. A field
dictionary of execution, risk, psychology, and market
microstructure. If you cannot define these terms precisely,
you cannot act precisely.

Intro — Read This Before You Begin

If you picked up this book looking for a few tips, you're in the wrong place.

This is not a beginner's guide.

This is not a motivational pamphlet with a few charts thrown in.

This is **the operating manual for surviving and dominating in the most unforgiving financial arena on Earth**.

Day trading is not a hobby.

It is not "passive income."

It is a combat sport played with money as the ammunition — and the other side has no mercy.

You're competing against professionals who have more experience, more capital, and more information than you.

The only reason you have a shot is because the market doesn't care about credentials — it cares about execution.

And execution is a learned skill.

But make no mistake: this book will not hold your hand.

Inside, you will:

- Strip away every retail-level habit that's costing you money.

- Learn how to operate like an institutional desk — even if you're trading from a laptop.

- Rewire your mental architecture so hesitation, fear, and revenge trading stop existing in your playbook.

- Build the systems that keep professionals profitable year after year, while amateurs blow up.

This is the **last trading book you will ever need** if you are serious about becoming a professional operator.

If you are not ready to hold yourself to that standard, close this book now.
If you are — then welcome to the other side.

Chapter 1 — The War You're Entering

Why 99% Never See the Real Battlefield

You have not been trading "the market."
You've been trading a **story** about the market—a tidy
movie of candlesticks and talking-head narratives designed
to keep you clicking while real decisions are made
elsewhere.

The real market isn't a chart. It's a **machine for moving
obligation**—benchmarks to hit, mandates to follow, hedges
to rebalance, basis to close, inventory to unwind, capital to
hide. Candles are the shadow on the wall. The hand making
the shapes belongs to people with calendars, constraints,
and lawyers.

Walk with me. We're going past the screensaver.

I. The Three Rooms

1) The Outer Room — Entertainment & Extraction

This is the public arena: price patterns packaged as
prophecy, "levels" treated like law, thumbnails screaming
in all caps. Its function is simple: **manufacture activity**.
Activity creates spreads, fees, and—most importantly—
liquidity for larger players to execute real business. When
you chase every break and fade every wick here, you are a
liquidity vendor. You're not trading; you're *feeding*.

2) The Middle Room — Skill Without Leverage

Serious retail, small funds, talented prop—in here,
competence lives. They know VWAP, delta, vPOC,
imbalance prints. They see traps more often than not. But
they're still **reactive** because they don't control the *why*. A
level breaks and they trade it; a tape stalls and they fade it.

1

They can make money—good money—but the room's ceiling is the absence of **sponsor insight**. They see the wave, not the tide table.

3) The Command Room — Sponsored Reality

In the inner room, price is a **by-product**. Decisions are made in terms of **benchmarks, constraints, and flows**:

- "We must finish this buyback under Rule 10b5-1 without lighting up the tape."

- "We're 48 bps behind our VWAP benchmark; switch to more aggressive child slices."

- "Gamma is deeply negative into Friday's expiry; hedge inventory before 2:30."

- "Close the month pinned near index weights; minimize slippage in the closing auction."

When you feel a "mysterious" push, someone is **completing a job**—not chasing your line on a five-minute chart.

II. The Cast You've Been Trading Against (and Didn't Know)

Forget "bulls vs bears." This battlefield is **constraints vs constraints**—capital organized by rule sets.

Long-Only Benchmarked Funds

They live and die by *relative performance* to VWAP or the index close. They don't "like" a price; they **need** a print inside tolerance. If you don't know when they must show their marks (close, month-end, quarter-end), you don't know when the tide turns from value-seeking to mark-seeking.

2

Quant Volatility Dealers & Options Market Makers

They are not making "calls." They are flattening **greeks**. If crowd positioning loads up on short-dated calls, dealers may be **short gamma**—forced buyers into strength, sellers into weakness. On certain days, your "breakout" is just a **hedge chase**. The chart didn't bless you; a book got balanced.

CTAs / Trend Followers / Risk-Parity

They scale mechanically with volatility and trend definitions. When realized vol compresses, they lever up; when it expands, they delever. They're the silent hand behind **grind days** and **air pockets**. You thought it was "low volume drift." It was a model dialing risk.

Corporate Executions (Buybacks, 10b5-1)

These flows are **legal, scheduled, and indifferent to your lines**—but they avoid spotlight. They'll layer passive bids, pull when you chase, and reload when you tire. If you've ever wondered why a stock refuses to die quietly for weeks —hi.

ETFs, Indexers, Rebalances

Creations/redemptions, adds/drops, monthly/quarterly reweights, FX hedges—**calendar-driven flows** that pin and unpin markets like clockwork. The close on those days isn't "random"; it's mechanical gravity.

HFT/Internalizers

They don't "believe" in levels; they monetize microstructure. They'll step in front of your orders, internalize retail flow, and flip it against lit venues at better economics. On a slow tape, they are the tape.

Discretionary Macro / Event Funds

They traffic in **asymmetry** around catalysts—policy, prints, breaks. When they commit, the move feels ordained. It's not. It's size meeting a vacuum you didn't map.

Each group has a **clock**, a **rulebook**, and a **boss**. When you grasp that, the market stops being "mood swings" and becomes a **timetable of obligations**.

III. The Venues & Pipes (Where the War Actually Happens)

If you only see lit exchanges, you're watching the parade from an alley.

- **Lit Books** (NYSE/Nasdaq): What the crowd sees. Good for signals, late for truth.

- **Dark Pools / ATS**: Size trades here to avoid moving price. If your lit breakout dies mysteriously, dark just fed.

- **Internalizers/Wholesalers**: Retail flow often never touches the exchange; it's priced against NBBO internally.

- **Auctions** (Open/Close): The **real** print that many benchmark to. Late-day violence? Someone's book is being judged at 3:59:59.

- **Order Types**: Reserve/iceberg, midpoint pegs, discretionary pegs, Hide-Not-Slide—you think you saw size; size was hiding.

Microstructure is not trivia. It's *how* the command room touches your screen.

IV. The Four Invisible Forces that Sculpt Your Candles

1. **Benchmarking Pressure**
   When the world reports against VWAP or the close, every deviation creates **urgency**. That urgency is why 3:30–4:00 pm can ignore your intraday theology. You were playing chess; they were racing a clock.

2. **Dealer Hedging & Gamma Regimes**
   Some days, dealers' hedges **suppress** volatility and magnetize price to big strikes ("pin risk"). Other days, their hedges **amplify** volatility (short gamma chases). If you don't ask, "What are dealers likely forced to do here?" you're arguing with physics.

3. **Liquidity Vacuums**
   Between high-volume nodes lie **dead zones**—air pockets where price can sprint on crumbs. A "shock" move often isn't news—it's your map missing a canyon.

4. **Calendar Gravity**
   Op-Ex, rebalance, earnings windows, blackout periods, quarter-end, month-end—**time** moves money. If your model ignores the calendar, your model ignores half the market.

V. The Narrative Machine (How Stories Weaponize Flow)

The story follows the flow, not the other way around. "Rates fell on X," "rallied on Y"—post-hoc comfort for people who need reason. The **command room** designs risk and then allows media to drape it in cause. Professionals treat narrative like **smoke color** in a wind tunnel: useful to see direction, irrelevant to engine thrust. Ask: *"Who did this story enable to finish their job?"* If you can't answer, you're holding the headline like a talisman.

VI. The Five Lies that Keep You Supplying Liquidity

Lie 1: Levels are laws.
They're magnets for stops and resting interest. Laws? No.
Convenient staging areas? Yes.

Lie 2: Volume confirms truth.
Volume confirms **who finished**. Real intent is seen in
where volume didn't move price (absorption) and **when** it
evaporated (exhaustion).

Lie 3: A breakout is bullish by definition.
A breakout is *buy orders executed*. Bullish only if
sponsorship persists after the print. If the sponsor was a
benchmark catch-up, the move can die right after the
gradebook closes.

Lie 4: The close is just the end.
For many participants, it's the **only** grade. The entire day
can be a preface.

Lie 5: Price is opinion.
Price is **balance sheet + calendar + constraint**. The tape is
a compliance document written in ticks.

VII. Case Files from the Command Room

A) The 10:17 Trap

Morning trend is up. Retail buys the third micro-pullback at
VWAP. At 10:17, a block sell prints, price dips, retail stops
get harvested. Then… immediate reclaim, stronger than
before.

What happened: a short, directed **liquidity raid** to fill a buy
program behind VWAP. Sponsor needed inventory; your
stops were the warehouse.

B) The Pin

Thursday into monthly Op-Ex. Price hovers within 0.2% of a giant strike. Breakouts fail, fades fail, everyone feels cursed.

What happened: **dealer long gamma** soaked both sides, re-hedging toward the strike. You tried to make narrative out of bounded mean reversion. The sponsor was math.

C) The 3:42 Squeeze

All day grind lower. At 3:42, tape flips vertical with offers vanishing. By the close, new HOD.

What happened: buy imbalance + benchmark urgency + intra-day under-positioning. The "trend day" was an **end-of-day inventory panic** into a grade. If you shorted because "down all day," you shorted a deadline.

D) The Vacuum Walk

Lunch lull. Price slips below a minor morning low and then falls five times as far as you'd expect on microscopic volume.

What happened: your profile map didn't mark a **low-volume ravine** created last week. The sponsor was **nothing** —that's the point. Empty zones accelerate.

VIII. The Operator's Questions (The Only Ones That Matter)

Before you click anything:

1. **Who is urgent here?**
   Benchmark-chasers? Dealers? CTAs? Corporates? If no one is urgent, odds of durable follow-through drop.

2.   What clock is running?
Op-Ex? Rebalance? Close? Earnings in blackout?
Which *time* forces action?

3.   Where is the next fuel?
Stops above/below? LVN gap? Auction
imbalance? If there is no fuel, there is no fire.

4.   What survives contact?
Not what flashed. What **stuck**. Which bids
stayed. Which offers refilled. Which move
persisted *after* the obvious point.

5.   Where am *I* in the food chain right now?
Be honest. Are you adding liquidity to someone
else's job—or harvesting the liquidity they
needed?

If you can't answer these, you are not trading—you're
volunteering.

IX. The Four Modes of the Inner Room (How Pros Actually "Think")

Mode 1: Surveillance
Watch, log, map, size the opposing inventory, mark the
vacuums. No hero trades. We are building **context
memory**.

Mode 2: Probe
Tiny risk to test reaction at the key hinge. We are buying
information: *How does price behave when we push? Who
hits back?* Small loss is tuition; fast confirmation is green
light.

Mode 3: Campaign
The thesis is alive; the sponsor agrees. We press into
strength, peel into obvious fuel stations, and stay until
structure, not fear, ends the play.

Mode 4: Extraction & Reset

Benchmarks met, fuel spent, microstructure tilts. We exit while others are still discovering the story. Then we **go dark**—no FOMO entries, no victory laps. Next job.

Most traders live only in Probe or full YOLO. Professionals rotate these modes with discipline. That's the difference.

X. The Operator's Oath (Pin This Above Your Screens)

I will trade *sponsorship*, not superstition.
I will respect the **clock** as much as the **level**.
I will read what **survives** contact, not what flashes.
I will map **fuel** before seeking fire.
I will embrace boredom as a position.
I will stop when *I* am compromised.
I will be the one who leaves the room with capital and clarity—every day.

XI. What Changes Starting Now

You are done being surprised by "random" moves. Starting now, you'll build your daily narrative from **sponsors, clocks, constraints, and maps**. The chart becomes a **report**, not a religion. Your job isn't to guess where price goes—your job is to know **who** has to act, **when**, and **where** the path of least resistance runs when they do.

When you think like this, you stop chasing. You stop fading out of boredom. You stop treating every candle like a confession. You become the operator who takes two trades a day and shakes your head at the chaos you used to call "opportunity."

You're through the door.

Chapter 2 — Mapping the Command Room

Position Before the Story, Exit Before the Crowd

Most traders think "institutions move the market" is just a phrase.
They've never thought through what that *actually means in process*.
They imagine a giant hand pushing price up or down, but that's a fantasy.

The reality is surgical. The "command room" doesn't move price by dumping millions of shares in one go — they *seed* price moves. They position early, using order flow and liquidity as camouflage, then build the story that retail will later chase.

If you want to step out of the outer layer and operate closer to the command room, you have to learn to map their positioning *before* the story breaks and *before* the liquidity rushes in.

Part 1 — Pre-Market Sponsor Recon

If the market is war, the pre-market is reconnaissance. By the time you wake up and open your platform, the command room has already made key decisions about where they want price *today*.

They do this through:

- Overnight futures positioning

- Block trades in the dark pools

- Pre-market volume anomalies in key tickers

- The alignment of correlated assets (e.g., ES vs. NQ divergence, sector rotation footprints)

Your mission in pre-market:
Identify *which sponsor is in control*. Is it accumulation sponsor, distribution sponsor, or liquidity harvest sponsor?

Here's how you spot it:

1. **Start with overnight futures structure**

   ° Did ES/NQ grind up slowly on low volume? That's *positioning*, not a breakout.

   ° Did they gap hard on thin liquidity? That's a *sentiment injection* — usually meant to fade early.

2. **Scan for block trade footprints**

   ° Look for unusually large prints in pre-market that don't match the visible liquidity on Level 2.

   ° These often mark where large players are *already* committing capital.

3. **Identify pre-market magnets**

   ° Key VWAP anchors from previous sessions

   ° Unfilled gaps from the past 2–3 days

   ° High-volume nodes on your composite profile

4. **Sector leadership confirmation**

- If tech leads pre-market and financials lag, know which index sponsor will control the open.

- No leadership = chop risk early.

By 9:20 a.m., you should have **one hypothesis** for the day: accumulation bias, distribution bias, or liquidity harvest bias.
If you can't make that call, you're already one step behind.

Part 2 — Intraday Sponsor Confirmation

The open is noise for most retail traders. They chase volatility without context.
Professionals use the first 30–45 minutes to confirm **which room is actually active**.

The difference between thinking it's "big money buying" and knowing it is the difference between a sniper and someone shooting in the dark.

Sponsor confirmation checklist:

1. **Opening Drive Behavior**

- Strong directional move with no meaningful pullback in first 5–10 minutes = sponsor initiative.

- Choppy overlapping candles = sponsor absent, algos in control.

2. **VWAP Interaction**

- Strong sponsor: price respects VWAP like a launchpad or ceiling.

      ○   Weak sponsor: price whips through VWAP multiple times early = no commitment yet.

3. **Volume Profile Development**

      ○   Watch the shape forming in the first hour. Bulging single node near extremes? Sponsor holding ground. Balanced, fat middle? Liquidity harvest in play.

4. **Correlation Confirmation**

      ○   If QQQ breaks out but ES/NQ diverge, sponsor is likely only partial — be careful.

By 10:15 a.m., you need your confirmation.
You are not guessing past this point.

Part 3 — Execution Translation

Once you know the sponsor bias, you don't take every trade in that direction.
You take only **the A+ liquidity moments** — the points where retail is most likely to hand over size without knowing it.

These moments occur in:

- VWAP reclaims or rejections with confirming volume

- Retests of overnight highs/lows after sponsor confirmation

- Traps where price runs one direction, sucks in late chasers, then reverses hard into sponsor bias

Execution law:
You do not chase the initial move.
You enter on *sponsor re-entry points*, where their position is defended, not created.

Part 4 — The Two-Trade Discipline

One of the biggest secrets from the command room:
Most professionals don't take 20 trades a day.
They take 1–3 that align perfectly with the sponsor bias, and they scale size accordingly.

The Two-Trade Discipline means:

- You commit to finding *only* the two cleanest, most confirmed moments of the day.

- If they never appear, you don't trade.

- If you hit one early and it's clean, you're done unless the second is equally strong.

This keeps you from bleeding capital on "almost" trades and forces you into patience mode — the mode professionals live in daily.

The Command Room Mindset Shift

The final shift here is psychological:
You're no longer thinking "I'm buying here because of a pattern."
You're thinking "I'm aligning my capital with the room that controls the day's narrative, and I'm getting out before they hand the story to retail."

That is the DNA of a professional operator.
And once you adopt it, you will see how much time and money you've wasted playing in the outer layer.

Chapter 3 — Liquidity Warfare

How the Market Hunts, Traps, and Transfers Capital Every Single Day

The Market's True Business Model

The market is not a place where buyers and sellers meet to "discover" price in a fair exchange. That's the marketing brochure for the public.

The market's true business model is **liquidity transfer** — moving capital from less-informed participants to more-informed participants through engineered price action.

That means that every spike, every stall, every "random" flush, is not random. It's part of a structural process designed to:

1. Create a story that pulls money in.

2. Build positions *against* that crowd.

3. Transfer liquidity at maximum efficiency with minimal market impact.

If you don't understand this, you're not trading *with* the market — you're trading *against* the house, in the outer layer.

Part 1 — Understanding Liquidity Zones

Every day, the market identifies *where* the money is hiding before it moves an inch.
These areas are called **liquidity zones**, and they exist at every timeframe:

- **Obvious highs/lows** from prior sessions

- **Round numbers** (whole-dollar or half-dollar levels)

- **Anchored VWAP points** from news or key opens

- **Large volume nodes** on a profile chart

Liquidity zones are where the stop orders, breakout orders, and pending limit orders stack up like dry powder.
The market's first objective is to *harvest* that liquidity — either to fill a real position or to fake one and reverse.

Professional law:
If you see price consolidating just below a liquidity zone with rising open interest and delta imbalance, someone's loading the gun.

Part 2 — The Two Types of Liquidity Hunts

Liquidity hunts are not all the same. Professionals differentiate them into:

1. True Break Hunts

- Purpose: To actually run through a liquidity zone and continue in that direction.

- Mechanics: Sponsors genuinely need to fill size, and the breakout gives them the liquidity to do it.

- Signature: Strong volume through the level, minimal wick, follow-through candles confirming control.

2. False Break Hunts (Stop Runs)

- Purpose: To *trigger* stops and breakout orders, then reverse against them.

- Mechanics: Sponsors use the orders at the zone to fill their *opposite* position.

- Signature: Sharp move through the level, heavy wick rejection, immediate drive back into range.

The problem? To retail traders, both look the same *until it's too late*.
The key is in the **context** before the hunt and the **reaction** after it.

Part 3 — Pre-Hunt Context Clues

Before any liquidity raid, the market sets the table:

1. **Compression Patterns**

   ○ Price coils into a tight range, pulling traders into smaller and smaller trades.

   ○ This loads both sides of the zone with stop liquidity.

2. **Delta Divergence**

   ○ Aggressive buying into a high but delta is flat or declining? That's passive sellers loading up to fade it.

3. **Volume Vacuum**

   ○ Sudden low volume into a key level often precedes a sharp liquidity raid.

   ○ This is the market "sucking in" before it strikes.

4.   **Index Correlation Asymmetry**

   ○   If ES is pushing a high but NQ lags,
           one of them is being used as a liquidity
           decoy.

Part 4 — The Execution Traps

Liquidity warfare is about *psychology in motion*. The traps
work because they weaponize natural human reactions:

- **The Breakout Trap** — Price rips through
  resistance, retail jumps long, sponsors sell into
  the rally and reverse.

- **The Flush Trap** — Sharp sell-off under support,
  shorts pile in, sponsors absorb and rip it back.

- **The VWAP Flip Trap** — Price rejects VWAP
  early, later reclaims with force, trapping shorts.

- **The Gap Fill Trap** — Price rushes to fill a prior
  gap, overshoots, then reverses hard.

The key is not avoiding all traps — it's **knowing which
side the sponsor is on before the trap triggers**.

Part 5 — Spotting the Sponsor in Real Time

Professionals don't guess after the fact.
They read **live sponsor behavior** in the tape, profile, and
VWAP structure.

Watch for:

- **Absorption** — Price stalls at a level despite
  aggressive buying/selling. Large passive orders
  are soaking up liquidity.

18

- **Initiative Drives** — Sudden acceleration *with* volume spikes from a balanced area.

- **Defensive Reclaims** — Sharp reclaim of VWAP or prior day's high/low after a false break.

The moment you see defensive reclaim after a trap, you're looking at a *sponsor protecting their position.* That's your cue to align.

Part 6 — Building the Liquidity Map Each Morning

Every day before the open:

1. Mark all obvious highs/lows from prior sessions.

2. Identify VWAP anchors from prior day and major news events.

3. Pull a composite profile for the past 5–10 days and mark high-volume nodes.

4. Set alerts at all these levels so you don't have to hunt mid-trade.

Your job is then to wait for the market to *hunt your map —* not the other way around.

Part 7 — The Exit Principle in Liquidity Warfare

Here's what most traders get wrong:
The moment your trade starts attracting *the same type of trader you're fading,* you're now in the danger zone.

Example:

- You catch a breakout early with sponsor confirmation.

- Ten minutes later, Twitter, Discord, and news squawk are all screaming the same breakout.

- That's your warning — you're now trading *with* the liquidity being targeted, not the room that set it up.

Professionals exit before the story is handed to the crowd.

Closing Mindset

If you reframe the market as a daily hunt for liquidity — not a fair auction — you immediately stop being the hunted.
You start thinking like a predator.
You know where the waterholes are.
You know which footprints mean prey and which mean a trap.

From here on, every trade you take must start with one question:
Whose liquidity am I using — and whose am I about to give away?

Chapter 4 — Supply & Demand: The Architecture of Control

Most traders draw boxes on charts and call them "zones." Professionals don't. To them, supply and demand are not rectangles — they are **inventory transfer layers**, born from the collision of sponsor constraints, liquidity hunts, and hidden order flow.

If you do not understand these layers, you will forever misread the battlefield. This chapter is not about marking levels — it is about decoding the structural truth of why price moves, where it pauses, and why it reverses.

Supply and demand is not a "strategy." It is the **architecture of control.**

Part I — What Supply & Demand Really Is

At its core, every market move is a negotiation between three forces:

1. **Inventory Requirement** — A sponsor must fill or exit size.

2. **Liquidity Availability** — Where opposing orders are clustered.

3. **Execution Camouflage** — How to complete the task without showing the hand.

When a sponsor discovers a patch of liquidity large enough to complete or anchor a task, that area becomes a **zone of significance**.

*   **Demand Zone:** Area where inventory was absorbed, creating a foundation for higher prints.

- **Supply Zone:** Area where inventory was unloaded, creating a ceiling for further advance.

These are not magic. They are footprints of sponsor activity.

Part II — The Three Types of Zones

Not all zones are equal. Professionals classify them with precision.

1. **Initiation Zones**

   ○ Created by explosive drives out of consolidation.

   ○ Signal where aggressive sponsorship entered with force.

   ○ Often re-tested because unfinished business remains.

2. **Continuation Zones**

   ○ Form mid-trend during pauses or shallow pullbacks.

   ○ Used by sponsors to add to winning positions.

   ○ Often ignored by retail, but crucial for campaign context.

3. **Exhaustion Zones**

   ○ Created at trend extremes with violent reversals.

○ The handoff point where sponsorship exits and retail takes the bag.

○ They look like "breakouts" until they collapse.

The operator's job is not to draw every box, but to **distinguish which type of zone you are observing** — initiation, continuation, or exhaustion.

Part III — Zone Mechanics (What Makes Them Real)

A true supply or demand zone has these structural elements:

- **Absorption Evidence** — Price held despite aggressive order flow. Large passive players were sitting there, taking the other side.

- **Imbalance Release** — The move away was decisive, one-sided, and left a volume vacuum behind it.

- **Liquidity Magnetism** — On return, price is drawn back because unfinished orders or trapped traders remain.

If these elements are absent, it is not a real zone — it is chart art.

Part IV — Sponsor Tactics at Zones

Sponsors don't treat zones as holy ground. They treat them as **tools**.

1. **Harvesting Opposite Orders**

○ At demand, they buy into panic selling.

○ At supply, they sell into euphoric buying.

2. **Creating False Security**

○ They let a zone hold just long enough for retail to believe it's safe, then run it deliberately to trigger stops and reload.

3. **Layered Defense**

○ True sponsor zones are rarely one-price deep. They are layered with hidden orders across several ticks or handles, designed to absorb gradually.

4. **Zone Engineering**

○ Sometimes zones are manufactured intentionally. Sponsors will "paint" a base, defend it visibly, then abandon it later, knowing the crowd will still respect it.

Part V — Reading Zone Context

A zone cannot be judged in isolation. Context is everything.

- **VWAP Relationship**
  Zones aligned with VWAP bias carry more weight. A demand zone below VWAP is often a trap; a demand zone reclaiming VWAP is true sponsorship.

- **Higher-Timeframe Liquidity**
  Zones that overlap with prior day/week highs or lows, option strikes, or high-volume nodes carry institutional magnetism.

- **Dealer Gamma Pressure**
  A supply zone above a giant call wall is more likely to hold. A demand zone near a put wall may act as structural support until expiry.

- **Auction Phase**
  In the Open, zones are often traps. Midday, they are build layers. Into the Close, they are staging for optics and risk transfer.

Part VI — How Zones Fail (The Operator's Edge)

The greatest edge is not knowing when zones hold — it's knowing when they are about to fail.

Failure signatures:

1. **Thin Return:** Price races back into a zone too quickly, signaling it is a magnet, not a fortress.

2. **Absorption Collapse:** On retest, passive orders vanish — price slices through without resistance.

3. **Flow Divergence:** Tape shows aggressive order flow aligned with the retest instead of against it.

4. **Calendar Conflict:** A zone sitting in front of major data or expiry is weaker than one aligned with sponsor timing.

Most retail blows up buying failed demand or shorting failed supply. Professionals profit because they understand **zones are conditional, not sacred.**

Part VII — Building the Operator's Zone Map

Each morning, your supply/demand prep must go beyond "drawing boxes."

Checklist:

- Mark only zones with clear absorption + imbalance.

- Note the type (initiation, continuation, exhaustion).

- Align each zone with VWAP, gamma strikes, and profile nodes.

- Tag each zone with probability rating (A, B, C).

- Track which sponsor archetype is most likely behind it (dealer defense, buyback bid, CTA add).

By 9:20 a.m., you should have a map that tells you not just *where* zones are, but *what role* they will play in today's war.

Part VIII — Live Case Files

Case A: The Phantom Demand Zone
Morning flush into a prior low. Price bounces hard. Retail calls it "demand." On retest, it slices through without pause. Why? Because the first bounce was only dealer hedging flow, not true sponsor absorption. No inventory base = no zone.

Case B: The Layered Supply Wall
Price grinds into a prior high all day, wicks out three times, never breaks clean. Retail shorts get chopped. Close slams lower. What happened? Corporate buyback program paused at that level all week, absorbing every uptick. That wall was real supply — hidden behind passive orders.

Case C: The Engineered Zone
Market builds a neat sideways base at midday. Everyone marks it as demand. Next morning, it gaps below and sells

off hard. What happened? Sponsors manufactured the zone to bait positioning, then yanked orders overnight. Manufactured "support" is a trap as old as the tape.

Closing Mandate

Supply and demand is not rectangles. It is the battlefield blueprint of inventory transfer. If you treat zones as patterns, you will be harvested. If you treat them as sponsor footprints — conditional, contextual, engineered — you will finally see the game as it is.

From this point forward, every zone you mark must answer three questions:

1. Whose inventory was here?

2. What unfinished business remains?

3. What calendar or flow force could flip it from fortress to failure?

Answer those, and you will never again mistake chart art for architecture.

Chapter 5 — The Cycle of Control

How Capital Rotates, Sentiment Resets, and Retail Is Trapped Across Timeframes

The Myth of Randomness

If Chapter 3 was about *intraday warfare*, Chapter 5 is about the **war campaign** — how the same core liquidity concepts are scaled up into multi-day and multi-week structures.

Markets don't just *happen*.
The same people who engineer intraday traps also **plan the larger sentiment arcs** that dictate how headlines are written, how analysts "discover" trends, and how retail sentiment swings from euphoria to despair and back again.

To survive, you must see the **phases** — because once you know which phase you're in, you know what kind of traps are being laid and what the true directional bias is behind the curtain.

Part 1 — The Four Phases of Sponsor Control

The cycle repeats again and again — in single stocks, indices, futures, crypto, FX.

Phase 1 — Accumulation (Sponsor Build)

- Price trades in a compressed range after a decline or long sideways period.

- Volume appears low to the untrained eye, but tape shows steady absorption.

- News is dead. No one's talking about it.

- Retail is either disinterested or convinced the asset is "dead money."

- This is where big money builds positions quietly.

Phase 2 — Expansion (Sponsor Release)

- Controlled push out of range with *sustainable* volume.

- News cycle begins to stir, analysts upgrade, headlines drip in.

- Early retail jumps in, creating liquidity for sponsors to add without chasing.

- Strong closes into highs, shallow pullbacks.

Phase 3 — Distribution (Sponsor Exit)

- Market pushes into extremes — overbought on every indicator, but keeps grinding.

- Headlines are euphoric. Retail believes "this time is different."

- Hidden in the grind: tape shifts to absorption *against* the move.

- Big blocks go off in dark pools or on upticks at the highs — sponsors quietly selling inventory to the latecomers.

Phase 4 — Liquidation (Sponsor Reset)

- News suddenly turns.

- Sharp drops through prior supports trigger stop cascades.

- Analysts downgrade, sentiment collapses.

- Retail sells in panic, often right back into sponsor bids.

- The cycle begins again at Accumulation.

Part 2 — Multi-Timeframe Liquidity Harvesting

In the intraday world, you saw liquidity hunts as quick spikes or traps.
In the multi-day cycle, those same mechanics are **drawn out**:

- **Accumulation phase** hunts liquidity *below* the base to shake out early longs.

- **Expansion phase** hunts liquidity *above* prior highs to force short covering.

- **Distribution phase** hunts even higher liquidity pools — FOMO breakout buyers — and fills sponsor exits.

- **Liquidation phase** hunts liquidity *below multiple swing lows* in a cascade to reload sponsor inventory.

Part 3 — Sentiment Engineering

Institutions don't just move price — they engineer **belief systems** in the crowd.

- **During Accumulation** — The story is boredom. "No catalyst." "Nothing to see here."

- **During Expansion** — The story is early promise. "Undervalued." "Smart money accumulating."

- **During Distribution** — The story is certainty. "Breakout to new highs coming." "Next big thing."

- **During Liquidation** — The story is doom. "Broken chart." "Sell everything."

Each narrative phase exists to **pull in the opposite side of the sponsor's trade**.

Part 4 — Detecting Phase Transitions in Real Time

Clues you're shifting phases:

1. **Shift in VWAP Behavior**

   - In Expansion: price rides above daily and weekly VWAP, reclaims quickly on dips.

   - In Distribution: price starts *failing* VWAP reclaims, grinding sideways instead of breaking clean.

2. **Profile Shape Changes**

   - Accumulation: fat, balanced profiles with high-volume nodes in the center.

   - Expansion: double-distribution days with value moving higher.

   - Distribution: skewed profiles with excess tails on the highs.

- ○ Liquidation: long, thin profiles with value dropping rapidly.

3. **Delta and Order Flow Shifts**

- ○ Watch for divergence: aggressive orders *into* highs without follow-through, or *into* lows without breakdown.

Part 5 — Why Retail Gets Trapped Every Time

Because retail trades the *visible story*, not the **phase context**.

- • In Accumulation: They're bored, they miss the low-risk entry.

- • In Expansion: They chase late, often after the first clear breakout.

- • In Distribution: They "buy the dip" into sponsor distribution.

- • In Liquidation: They panic sell at the lows into sponsor re-accumulation.

This isn't incompetence — it's **by design**. The market is structured to make the visible story the *opposite* of the real one.

Part 6 — The Swing-Intraday Connection

Here's the key to making this usable:
Every phase contains **intraday mini-cycles** that
mirror the larger phase.

Example:

- In a larger Distribution phase, you'll see
  daily intraday expansions *up* that trap longs
  by the close.

- In a larger Accumulation phase, you'll see
  intraday flushes down into sponsor bids that
  reverse sharply.

That's why intraday traders who align their trades
with the higher phase have a dramatically higher win
rate — they're swimming in the same current as the
campaign.

Part 7 — Using the Cycle of Control in Your Trading

Daily routine:

1. Identify the phase on the *higher timeframe*
   (daily / weekly).

2. Map liquidity zones relevant to that phase.

3. Execute intraday trades *in harmony* with the
   phase bias.

If you're in Expansion, you fade breakdowns and join reclaims.

If you're in Distribution, you fade breakouts and sell failed reclaims.

If you're in Liquidation, you fade panic flushes and buy sponsor reclaims.

Closing Mindset

Once you see the market as a **multi-timeframe campaign**, you stop treating trades as isolated events. You understand the *why* behind every push and every pullback. You stop fearing the market — because you know what game is being played, and more importantly, **whose turn it is to lose**.

Chapter 6 — The Options Overhang: How Gamma Flow Dictates the Tape

Why This Chapter Matters

If you've ever watched a "breakout" grind to a halt at a random number, or a selloff suddenly freeze and reverse in a dead zone, you weren't watching "price action." You were watching option dealers hedge their books.

Options positioning is the invisible hand steering the underlying — not because dealers want to "move" the market, but because their risk models force them to. Understanding gamma flow is the institutional stamp of credibility that separates amateurs playing candle patterns from professionals anticipating the physics of the tape.

This chapter will arm you with the x-ray vision to see how options dictate equity movement intraday, daily, and around expiries.

Part 1 — The Dealer's Job (And Why You Must Care)

Dealers sell options to the crowd. Their business model is simple: collect premium, stay hedged.
That "stay hedged" part is where your charts live or die.

- **Long Gamma vs. Short Gamma**

    ○ *Long Gamma:* Dealer hedges by selling strength and buying weakness → suppresses volatility, pins price near strikes.

    ○ *Short Gamma:* Dealer hedges by buying strength and selling weakness → amplifies volatility, accelerates moves away from strikes.

○ **Delta Hedging 101**
Every option position carries delta
exposure. Dealers neutralize it in the
underlying. When retail piles into calls,
dealers are short gamma → every uptick
forces them to buy stock, fueling the rally.
When retail piles into puts, dealers may
need to dump stock into weakness, creating
cascades.

You think you're trading a breakout. You're trading dealer
math.

Part 2 — Pin Risk and Magnet Strikes

Ever noticed price stick like glue to a strike into Friday's
close? That's not random "market indecision" — that's
gamma pinning.

- **High Open Interest Strikes** act as magnets.

- Dealers lean on hedges to keep their books flat →
  price oscillates around that strike like iron filings
  around a magnet.

- On expiration Friday, this effect amplifies —
  every tick through the strike changes dealer
  hedge demand, reinforcing the pin.

Pro Law: If you don't map the OI landscape every week,
you're trading blind to the strongest gravitational force in
equities.

Part 3 — How Gamma Shapes Intraday

Intraday price behavior shifts based on whether the market
is in a long or short gamma regime:

- **Long Gamma Environment:**

  - Expect choppy, mean-reverting price action.

  - Breakouts fade quickly.

  - VWAP becomes an even stronger gravity center.

- **Short Gamma Environment:**

  - Expect violent directional moves.

  - Stops cascade faster.

  - Liquidity vacuums are amplified — once price enters thin zones, dealers accelerate the move with forced hedges.

Tell: Watch the pace of reversion vs. acceleration. If every breakout stalls, you're in long gamma. If every push snowballs, you're in short gamma.

Part 4 — The Expiry Engine

The calendar is everything. Options expiration is not just a date — it's a risk reset.

- **Monthly Opex (third Friday):** The largest structural flow event in equities. Billions in notional exposure reset.

- **Quarterly "Triple Witching":** Futures + index options + single-stock options expire together → violent rebalancing.

- **Post-Opex Weeks:** Volatility often releases after dealers shed hedges.

Playbook:

- Into expiry → look for pinning near large strikes.

- Post-expiry → expect volatility release in whichever direction positioning was bottling energy.

Part 5 — The Gamma Flip Zones

Key concept: dealers flip behavior when price crosses certain strikes.

- Above a big call wall → forced buying amplifies upside.

- Below a big put wall → forced selling cascades downside.

These "flip zones" explain why moves suddenly accelerate after sitting flat for hours. It wasn't "sentiment." It was the math flipping.

Part 6 — Tactical Applications for the Operator

You don't need a PhD in derivatives to use this. Here's how pros integrate gamma flow daily:

1. **Map the OI Landscape Pre-Market**

   ◦ Identify largest strikes on your ticker(s).

   ◦ Note where gamma flips from long to short.

- ◦ **Adjust Expectations**

- ◦ Long gamma → fade breakouts, scalp mean reverts.

- ◦ Short gamma → ride expansions, trail stops wider.

2. **Anchor Your Liquidity Map to Strikes**

- ◦ Treat high OI strikes like liquidity pools.

- ◦ Expect raids above/below them, especially near expiry.

4. **Clock Awareness**

- ◦ Friday afternoons: pin risk dominates.

- ◦ Post-expiry Mondays: freed volatility.

5. **Overlay With VWAP**

- ◦ VWAP + strike magnet = sponsor's strongest gravity zones.

Part 7 — Case Files of Gamma in Action

- **Tesla $700 Pin (Opex Friday):** Price oscillated in a $5 band for six hours, ignoring every macro headline. That wasn't "indecision" — it was dealers long gamma at the $700 strike, hedging both sides.

- **SPY Short Gamma Cascade (March Selloff):** Break of 400 triggered dealer put hedges, forcing sells into a thin zone. What looked like "panic" was just risk math.

- **Apple Breakout Reversal:** Call-heavy OI made dealers short gamma. Price ripped $3 intraday, only to fade as hedges unwound. Retail saw "manipulation." Professionals saw a gamma unwind.

Part 8 — The Operator's Gamma Checklist

Before every session, ask:

- Where is the largest OI concentration?

- Are dealers long or short gamma at today's price?

- Where are the flip zones?

- What's the calendar — are we approaching Opex or just past it?

- How will this gamma regime affect my trade selection?

If you don't know these answers, you are trading with half the battlefield map missing.

Closing Mandate

Gamma is not optional knowledge. It is the silent architect of price. Every intraday trap, every Friday pin, every violent unwind has its roots in the options market.

Professionals don't just watch the chart. They watch the book that dictates the chart. Until you integrate gamma flow into your daily process, you're still playing the outer game. Once you do, you'll see the tape bend exactly where the math says it must — and you'll stop calling it "random."

Chapter 7 — The Sponsor's Playbook: Inside the Daily War Room

Institutional Architecture + U.S. Equities Tactical Execution

The Truth About the Daily Auction

If you could sit in the actual war room of an institutional trading desk — hedge fund, prop desk, or a market-making operation — you'd see one thing very clearly:
They are not guessing.

Most traders think they're "in the market."
They're not.
They're in a daily *auction* run by sponsors — the people who have the capital and order flow to dictate **where** price goes, **when** it gets there, and **how much liquidity is left in the path**.

Sponsors are not "trend followers." They are **inventory managers**.
They move price to create the conditions they need to fill or unload positions without destroying their own executions.

Every move is **sequenced**. Every hour of the trading day has a **primary mission**.
They don't "see what happens" — they **create** what happens.

The goal of this chapter is to **strip away the mystery** and lay out their operational flow *in order*, so you can mirror it, anticipate it, and stop being the liquidity they feed on.

If you want to survive in their world, you must:

1. Know **which phase of the day** you're in.

2. Know **what sponsors are trying to accomplish** in that phase.

3. Trade in alignment with that **phase objective**, not your feelings.

Phase 1 — Overnight Positioning (Global Sweep)

Time Window: Post-close to U.S. pre-market.
Sponsor Objective: Shape the battlefield before the main auction opens.

Mechanics

*   **Inventory Adjustment:** Sponsors use global sessions (Asia, Europe) to lighten or add size where retail participation is minimal.

*   **Sentiment Tilt:** Overnight headlines — earnings previews, guidance tweaks, rumor flows — are *strategic releases* to frame sentiment before volume arrives.

*   **Liquidity Location:** They map prior day's highs/lows, VWAP, settlement price, and overnight range extremes.

U.S. Tactical Translation

*   **4:00–8:00 PM ET:** Post-market block crosses and late prints reveal hidden sponsor transactions.

*   **4:00 AM ET onwards:** Pre-market is thin. Any grind into a prior-day liquidity pool is often a *reverse setup* for the main open.

43

Retail Trap

Thinking overnight moves are "real." Most are manufactured to set up the opposite main session move.

Phase 2 — Pre-Market Reconnaissance

Time Window: 8:30–9:29 AM ET.
Sponsor Objective: Finalize the day's first trap.

Mechanics

- **Economic Data Shakes:** 8:30 AM releases often create fake direction to lure bias.

- **Level Confirmation:** Overnight levels are confirmed or discarded; opening targets are chosen.

- **Sentiment Read:** Order book tilt, pre-market volume concentration, and options OI shifts reveal where retail is leaning.

U.S. Tactical Translation

- Pre-market VWAP vs. prior day VWAP is key — dislocations often revert.

- Identify the first liquidity magnets: overnight high/low, prior day high/low, and any gap zone.

Retail Trap

Pre-market breakouts that look clean rarely survive the first 15 minutes of main session liquidity.

Phase 3 — The Open Sequence (Trap Deployment)

Time Window: 9:30–10:30 AM ET.
Sponsor Objective: Secure control of the auction by forcing early commitment from the wrong side.

Mechanics

- **False Breaks:** Drive price beyond overnight extremes, trigger stops, then reverse.

- **VWAP Games:** First touch of VWAP is often rejection bait. A clean reclaim is rare in the first minutes.

- **Volume Front-Loading:** Massive prints in the first 5–15 minutes create commitment.

U.S. Tactical Translation

- Watch for "high-volume wick" bars that reverse — they mark sponsor stop raids.

- A real directional move often begins between 9:45–10:15 after inventory alignment is complete.

Retail Trap

Chasing the first move out of the gate without understanding it's often an engineered test, not the trend.

Phase 4 — Midday Positioning (The Quiet Kill)

Time Window: 11:00 AM–1:30 PM ET.
Sponsor Objective: Build or unwind size without disrupting the market.

Mechanics

- **Thin Liquidity Drift:** Price stays in tight channels to hide large execution.

- **Passive Absorption:** Sponsors fill size passively as retail churns.

- **VWAP Anchoring:** Midday holds above or below VWAP hint at sponsor bias.

U.S. Tactical Translation

- Repeated VWAP taps with no break are accumulation/distribution tells.

- Low volatility does not mean "nothing is happening" — it's often where the real build occurs.

Retail Trap

Overtrading the midday drift, getting chopped out while sponsors quietly set up the afternoon move.

Phase 5 — Power Hour (The Hammer Drop)

Time Window: 3:00–4:00 PM ET.
Sponsor Objective: Lock in inventory, control the closing print, and set up tomorrow's trap.

Mechanics

- **Closing Level Control:** Push into breakouts to lure overnight longs, or slam into lows to scare holders.

- **Auction Risk Transfer:** Massive blocks move in the closing auction without spooking intraday charts.

- **Next-Day Narrative Planting:** Closing extremes create the context for overnight news releases.

U.S. Tactical Translation

- If price closes above a breakout level with volume, expect sponsors to use overnight to offload to retail buyers.

- If it closes at the lows, expect a relief push early the next day — often into another trap.

Retail Trap

Interpreting the close as the "final word" on trend instead of the setup for tomorrow's manipulation.

Black Book Commandments from the Sponsor's Playbook

1. **Every phase has an objective — trade the objective, not the noise.**

2. **VWAP is the central gravity — sponsors orbit around it, not chase it.**

3. **Overnight moves are staging grounds, not finished plays.**

4. **Midday is when the biggest positions are built — invisibly.**

5. **The close is the lie told to the next day's traders.**

Chapter 8 — The Sponsor Archetypes Playbook: Decoding the Forces Behind the Tape

Every trader sees candles. Few ask *whose job the candle represents*. Price is not opinion — it is the by-product of sponsors executing mandates under constraints. If you can identify which archetype is active, the entire day stops looking "random" and collapses into predictable behaviors.

This playbook is your field manual. Treat it like the operator's Rosetta Stone. Each archetype comes with:

- **Identity:** What they are, what constraints bind them.

- **Signature:** How they leave fingerprints in the tape.

- **Trap:** How their flow deceives and harvests retail.

- **Operator Play:** How you align or fade when they're in control.

Archetype 1: The Long-Only Benchmark Fund

- **Identity:** Mutual funds, pensions, asset managers. Bound to benchmarks (VWAP, closing print). Must show compliance.

- **Signature:**

    ○ Relentless passive flow near VWAP.

- ○ Urgent pushes in the final 30 minutes to "make the grade."

- ○ Rarely initiates; they complete.

- **Trap:** Retail thinks the 3:30 surge is "breakout momentum." In reality, it's just a report card.

- **Operator Play:** Fade their urgency if it runs into exhaustion. Or pre-position early when you know they'll need to chase the close.

Archetype 2: The Dealer / Options Market Maker

- **Identity:** They are not "trading ideas." They are hedging books. Gamma exposure dictates whether they are volatility suppressors or amplifiers.

- **Signature:**

  - ○ Pin risk around option strikes into Op-Ex.

  - ○ Sudden acceleration when short gamma — forced to buy highs, sell lows.

  - ○ Gravity back to strikes when long gamma — every breakout dies.

- **Trap:** Retail believes breakouts/fakeouts are "news driven." Dealer hedging explains 80% of it.

- **Operator Play:** Always ask: is the dealer long gamma (expect compression, fades) or short gamma (expect violence)? Align trades with hedging regime, not chart patterns.

Archetype 3: The CTA / Trend Follower / Risk Parity Machine

- **Identity:** Systematic players scaling risk up/ down mechanically. Inputs: realized vol, trend definitions.

- **Signature:**

    ◦ Slow, grinding directional moves with minimal retrace.

    ◦ Air pockets when vol expands (forced deleveraging).

    ◦ Correlated flows across indices and asset classes.

- **Trap:** Retail sees "smooth trend" and assumes conviction. In reality, it's levered positioning that can unwind mechanically with zero warning.

- **Operator Play:** Ride their grind if aligned. Exit fast when volatility flips, because they will puke size into nothing.

Archetype 4: The Corporate Execution (Buybacks, 10b5-1 Programs)

- **Identity:** Corporate treasuries reducing float. Programs run under compliance rules, executed by brokers with stealth.

- **Signature:**

    ◦ Relentless bid in the background for weeks.

- ○ Low volatility drift upward, resistant to selling pressure.

- ○ Pauses during blackout windows.

- **Trap:** Retail thinks the stock is "strong" for technical reasons. It's just corporate liquidity absorption. When blackout hits, support vanishes.

- **Operator Play:** Align with buyback support during active windows. Stand aside during blackout gaps.

Archetype 5: The ETF / Index Rebalancer

- **Identity:** Calendar-driven flows. Mechanical, not discretionary.

- **Signature:**

    - ○ Sharp end-of-day moves tied to reweights.

    - ○ Apparent "random" gaps around quarterly/monthly closes.

    - ○ Cross-asset hedging pressure from FX when foreign flows rebalance.

- **Trap:** Retail sees "breakout failure." It was never a breakout — it was an ETF add/remove.

- **Operator Play:** Mark calendar rebalances. Expect magnetism to index weights and violent closes. Fade the "trend" if it's just mechanical.

Archetype 6: The HFT / Internalizer

- **Identity:** Speed predators. Profit from microstructure, not direction.

- **Signature:**

    ○ Flickering quotes, vanishing liquidity.

    ○ Choppy, whipsaw moves in midday when no sponsor is active.

    ○ Spreads tighten/loosen aggressively with volatility shifts.

- **Trap:** Retail overtrades chop days, thinking there's a trend. In reality, it's internalizers recycling flow.

- **Operator Play:** Recognize chop = HFT regime. Reduce size, or stand down. Save ammo for when real sponsors enter.

Archetype 7: The Discretionary Macro / Event Fund

- **Identity:** Big bets on catalysts — policy, data, geopolitics.

- **Signature:**

    ○ Quiet positioning → sudden asymmetric move at event.

    ○ Size accelerates into vacuum — feels "ordained."

    ○ Willing to sit flat for weeks, then strike once.

- ○ **Trap:** Retail mistakes the move as "organic." It was triggered by one decision + vacuum.

- **Operator Play:** Respect calendar catalysts. Pre-map fuel zones. If they strike, align fast or don't play. Never fade their urgency.

Archetype 8: The Narrative Planting Desk

- **Identity:** Not a flow, but a force. PR, media, rumor desks. They frame crowd bias to set up liquidity harvest.

- **Signature:**

  - ○ Overnight news drips before sponsor positioning.

  - ○ Midday rumor drops to disrupt drift.

  - ○ "Cause" headlines after moves that were already engineered.

- **Trap:** Retail trades the headline. Pros ask: "Whose inventory did this headline enable?"

- **Operator Play:** Treat narrative as smoke. Follow the flow that preceded it.

How to Use the Archetype Map

Every day, ask: *Which sponsor archetype is most urgent right now?*

- **If benchmark funds → expect closing flows.**
  Example: Watch for sudden urgency between 3:30–4:00 p.m. as funds push price toward VWAP or the close to meet their

benchmarks. A quiet tape can flip into heavy imbalances purely for marking purposes.

• If dealers → map gamma regime.
Example: On long gamma days, breakouts stall and mean-revert; on short gamma days, every push accelerates violently. The option positioning tells you whether to fade or ride momentum.

• If CTAs → respect grind or unwind.
Example: In calm, vol-suppressed markets, expect slow directional "melt-ups" as CTAs lever up. When volatility spikes, expect sharp air pockets as they unwind size mechanically.

• If corporates → lean into quiet bid.
Example: A buyback program often creates a steady underlying bid. This explains why a stock refuses to die quietly — support is artificial and persists until blackout windows.

• If ETF rebalances → mark calendar dates.
Example: On rebalance days, end-of-session prints can swing hard as funds adjust index weights. Moves that look "random" are simply calendar-driven order flow.

• If HFTs → chop filter on.
Example: Midday churn with flickering quotes and no follow-through is often HFT-dominated. Expect tight whipsaws, not trend — size down or stand aside until sponsorship returns.

• If macro funds → calendar catalyst ready.
Example: Ahead of Fed announcements, CPI prints, or geopolitical events, discretionary macro funds position quietly, then strike big on release. Expect asymmetry, not balance.

• If narrative desks → trade the flow, not the story.
Example: Overnight rumor drops or midday news bursts rarely start the move — they justify moves already underway. Anchor to the flow that preceded the headline.

Chapter 9 — The Mind of the Professional: Psychological Architecture for Day Traders

Why This Chapter Matters More Than Any Strategy

Every losing trader I've ever met has blamed their system, their broker, the market, or the "algos." But when you dig deeper, their real problem is *execution under psychological pressure*. Strategy only works when it is filtered through the mental operating system of a professional. If your OS (operating system) is corrupted, every decision is infected — no matter how "perfect" the setup.

Mental Operating Systems: Amateur vs. Professional

- **Amateur OS**: Runs on impulse. Every piece of news, every tick in price, every trade idea from Twitter is processed as if it needs immediate action. They *feel* the market and then act.

- **Professional OS**: Runs on conditional logic. Every input is processed through "Does this fit my predefined conditions?" If not, it's discarded instantly without regret or FOMO.

You can spot the difference instantly: Amateurs explain their trades with feelings ("It looked strong," "I thought it would…"). Professionals explain theirs with frameworks ("It met criteria X, Y, Z and confirmed on metric Q").

The Identity Gap: From Trader to Capital

Until you stop thinking like a "person trying to make money" and start thinking like *capital deploying itself*, you will fight yourself on every trade.

- **Trader thinking**: "I need to make back what I lost yesterday."

- **Capital thinking**: "Is the expected value of this deployment high enough to justify risk today?"

When you see yourself as capital:

1. Risk tolerance is a fixed property, not an emotion.

2. You deploy only in favorable terrain; you don't try to "force" gains.

3. You understand that some days, standing still is compounding — because *not losing is making money over time*.

Emotional Compression: Control the Swings or Be Controlled by Them

Your brain is hardwired to exaggerate the emotional intensity of gain and loss. In trading, this distortion destroys decision quality. The pro's job is to *flatten* those spikes in real-time.

Compression Techniques:

- **Pre-Trade Containment**: Every position is entered with a fully pre-defined stop, target, and size — so no in-trade math is needed.

- **Loss Normalization**: Accept in advance that X% of trades *will* be losers, even in winning months.

- **Win Neutralization**: Log a win, note the data, and return to zero-state. Do not inflate ego between trades.

If your mental state after a big win is anything other than neutral readiness, you're already in danger.

Decision Fatigue: The Hidden Saboteur

The human brain has a finite number of high-quality decisions it can make each day. In day trading, where conditions change rapidly, decision quality degrades faster than you think.

Pro Methods to Manage Fatigue:

- **Set Execution Windows**: Define exact time ranges you will take trades (e.g., 9:30–11:15, 1:30–3:15). Outside those windows, you only observe.

- **Simplify Universe**: Only trade the same small set of instruments — know their rhythm better than anyone else.

- **Pre-Load Scenarios**: Do your thinking before the market opens. Intraday should be 80% execution, 20% adaptation.

Decision fatigue is why pros often make the day's best trade early — and why amateurs give it back in the afternoon.

The Institutional Mindset Shift

You cannot beat the market reacting tick-for-tick to price. Institutions operate on structured *if–then* logic, probability, and position management over time.

Adopt their habits:

- Build a **daily battle plan**: 3–4 core scenarios you expect, plus how you will act in each.

- Track **flow and context** over signals. A "buy" signal in a selling day is trash; a "sell" signal in a strong trend is a trap.

- Think in **campaigns**: one trade may be part of a 3–5 trade sequence over days/weeks in the same instrument.

The Self-Override Protocol

Every trader hits that moment: hand hovering over the buy/sell button knowing they are breaking their own rules. Amateurs negotiate with themselves. Pros execute the override.

Three-Step Override:

1. **Recognize Your Tell** — racing pulse, shallow breathing, hyper-focus on one candle.

2. **Physically Interrupt** — stand, push chair back, change visual focus.

3. **Re-Center** — ask: "Am I acting as capital or as a person chasing?"

You will not always win the mental battle *before* the urge arises. But you can train to cut the circuit *after* recognition — and that is often enough to prevent catastrophic trades.

Building a Bulletproof Trading Mindset

By combining all of the above:

- Identity alignment (*I am capital*).

- Emotional compression (flatten the spikes).

- Decision fatigue control (preserve energy for high-quality execution).

- Institutional mindset shift (scenarios and campaigns).

- Self-override (stop the bleed before it starts).

You are no longer operating as "a trader trying to win." You are operating as **a capital deployment mechanism** — deliberate, controlled, and scalable.

That is the architecture that allows a day trader to survive *and* thrive long enough to make serious wealth.

Chapter 10 — Capital & Risk Mastery: The Rules of Deployment

The Law That Separates Survivors from Casualties

In every prop floor, hedge fund desk, and institutional war room, there's one law that never gets broken:
You deploy capital to survive first, grow second.

Amateurs flip that order — they chase growth first, and then wonder why they blow up. Pros understand that growth is a *side effect* of survival. Without survival, there is no compounding, and without compounding, there is no lasting wealth.

The Capital Deployment Pyramid

Your capital must be segmented into three functional tiers:

1. **Core Preservation Layer** – The "oxygen tank." This is the base you never drain. If you lose this, the game is over.

2. **Operational Deployment Layer** – This is the working capital you use to generate returns in normal conditions.

3. **Aggression Layer** – A small, high-risk tranche used only in optimal conditions with proven edge.

If you mix these layers — if you start trading your oxygen tank as if it's aggression capital — you've already signed your own death certificate.

Risk Per Trade: Non-Negotiable Rule

Professionals never think in "dollars I want to make." They think in **percent of risk capital I'm willing to lose if wrong**.

The pro standard:

- **0.5% to 1%** of total risk capital per trade.

- Scaling up risk *only* when equity curve and win rate confirm stability over months.

- Cutting risk in half or more during drawdown phases.

The purpose of the rule is not to limit upside — it's to ensure that no single trade or bad streak can destroy months or years of work.

Scaling In and Out Like a Professional

Retail traders scale in randomly ("it's going up, I'll add"). Pros scale in **pre-planned** and scale out **strategically**.

Scaling In Rules:

- Only add *if* market action continues to confirm the original thesis.

- Each add must be smaller than the initial core position — never pyramid into weakness.

Scaling Out Rules:

- Partial exits at pre-identified structural levels (VWAP reclaim, liquidity pockets, prior highs/lows).

• Keep a runner only if the day's volatility and trend behavior justify it.

Scaling is not about greed — it's about maximizing efficiency while protecting the core profit already earned.

Drawdown Survival Protocol

Every trader will face a drawdown. The difference between pros and blow-ups is **how they respond**.

The pro playbook:

1. **Cut size** immediately — even if the drawdown is "small."

2. **Stop strategy hopping** — return to the core playbook that produced previous gains.

3. **Tighten execution windows** — focus only on your highest-probability time-of-day or conditions.

A drawdown is not the time to make back losses quickly — it's the time to *restore stability*.

Aggressive Growth Windows

There *are* moments when pros push harder — when everything lines up:

• Volatility is elevated but clean.

• Their specific setups are firing with high frequency and win rate.

• Market structure is aligning across multiple timeframes.

During these windows:

- Size may be increased up to **double** normal risk.

- Multiple correlated trades may be taken *only* if risk is distributed intelligently.

- The moment the data shifts, aggression stops — no clinging to "I was killing it last week."

Aggression is always **temporary** and **data-driven**, not emotional.

The Institutional Risk Lens

Institutions view every trade through three simultaneous lenses:

1. **Trade Risk** — the defined loss if wrong.

2. **Portfolio Risk** — total exposure across all open positions.

3. **Strategic Risk** — impact of the trade on overall objectives (monthly, quarterly).

Retail traders almost always think only in terms of Trade Risk — and that's why they blow up when several "independent" trades all fail together.

The Capital Deployment Commandments

1. **Capital is Ammunition — Never Fire Blind**

2. **Survival > Growth — Every Single Day**

3. **Risk Is Pre-Defined or You Don't Enter**

4.   **Size Follows Data, Not Ego**

5.   **Cut Faster, Scale Slower**

6.   **Aggression Is Earned, Not Default**

7.   **Drawdowns Are Managed, Not Avoided**

With this, the trader is now armed with **the same capital and risk architecture used on real institutional desks** — stripped of fluff, stripped of retail myths, boiled down to principles that actually keep you in the game long enough to become truly wealthy.

Chapter 11 — The Flow Advantage: Understanding Liquidity and Market Energy

The Invisible Map You're Trading On

Every tick you see on a chart is the aftermath of a liquidity event — somebody hit the bid, lifted the offer, or absorbed a block.
But what you don't see, unless you've trained your eyes, is *where the liquidity sits before it's triggered.*

Professional traders don't just "look for setups" — they trade **against the liquidity map**, the same way a predator hunts against the migration patterns of its prey. If you only watch price, you're already late. If you watch liquidity, you're watching the future.

Why Price Moves

Forget the retail fairytale that price moves "because buyers outnumber sellers." That's like saying the ocean's tide changes "because more water wants to go north than south."

Price moves when:

1. **Resting liquidity is removed** — Large buy or sell orders get hit and vanish.

2. **Aggressive liquidity enters** — Market orders consume whatever is in front of them, forcing repricing.

3. **Absorption breaks** — A player who was stopping price decides to stop absorbing, letting the market slide.

When you understand these three causes, you stop being surprised by sudden reversals or "fake" breakouts — because you're no longer reacting to the candle, you're reacting to the energy behind it.

Liquidity Pools and Kill Zones

Every market has areas where liquidity clusters — prior highs/lows, VWAP, round numbers, obvious technical levels, option strike prices, etc.
These are not "magical" — they are simply where orders stack.

The Two Kill Zones:

- **Above Obvious Highs** — Where stops from shorts and breakout buys live side-by-side.

- **Below Obvious Lows** — Where stops from longs and breakdown sells cluster.

Institutions will target these areas *even if* they don't intend to reverse there — sometimes just to trigger a flush of orders to fill their real size.

Energy Transfer in the Market

Think of liquidity as energy waiting to be released. A breakout that triggers stops releases a burst of energy in one direction — if absorbed, that energy gets *redirected* into the opposite direction.

This is why you'll often see:

- **False breakouts** → violent reversals.

- **VWAP touches** → aggressive reclaims or rejections.

- **Post-news spikes** → fade moves once initial orders are filled.

The key is to stop thinking "trend" and start thinking **energy flow**: Where is it building? When will it release? In which direction will it sustain?

Institutional Liquidity Triggers

There are three main ways big players intentionally release liquidity:

1. **Stop Runs** — Forcing a flush to fill positions at better prices.

2. **Liquidity Gaps** — Trading into thin areas to trigger panic or chase.

3. **Absorption Withdrawal** — Pulling a large bid/ offer suddenly so price free-falls or spikes.

Once you know these plays, you'll start spotting them daily — and you'll realize that most "random" market moves are nothing of the sort.

The Flow Advantage in Execution

When you align your trade entries with the liquidity map:

- Your entries are earlier and tighter.

- Your stop losses are smaller but safer.

- Your profit targets hit faster because you're positioned *before* the crowd.

Retail trades *after* the energy release. Pros trade *into* the release.

Building Your Own Liquidity Map

Even without a Level 3 order book, you can build a mental liquidity map by:

- Marking **obvious prior highs/lows** on your chart.

- Identifying **VWAP and standard deviation bands**.

- Noting **round numbers** and **key option strikes**.

- Watching **volume profile nodes** for heavy prior activity.

Then ask: If I were a large player, where would I need price to go to fill my order without moving the market too much? That's where the real game is happening.

The Psychological Edge of Flow Awareness

When you know where liquidity is and why price moves, you stop feeling "attacked" by the market.
You stop blaming "fake outs" and "manipulation" and instead start seeing it as *orchestration*.
And once you see the orchestration, you can choose to be part of the orchestra — not the audience.

Chapter 12 — Precision Timing: The Professional's Clock

Why Time is a Weapon in Day Trading

Amateurs think the market is a continuous stream of "opportunities" from the open bell to the close. Professionals know the truth: **time of day determines probability**.

The market is not random throughout the session — it breathes in *predictable volatility cycles*. Your odds of catching a clean move are not the same at 9:45 AM as they are at 1:30 PM. If you treat all hours equally, you're shooting into the dark.

The Three Core Volatility Windows

1. **The Opening Drive (9:30–10:15 AM EST)**

   ○ Highest liquidity influx from overnight positioning, premarket orders, and market-on-open imbalance.

   ○ Sharpest, cleanest momentum moves happen here — but also the fastest failures.

   ○ Professionals use this window to **set the day's tone** — not to force every trade. Sometimes the best move is to watch, map the liquidity, and only strike when your edge is clear.

2.   **The Midday Drift (11:00 AM–1:30 PM)**

   ◦   Liquidity thins, algos dominate, and
       trends stall or chop.

   ◦   Institutional players are rebalancing,
       not initiating size.

   ◦   This is where retail gets chopped up —
       pros either stand down or trade micro-
       scalps with defined liquidity traps.

3.   **The Power Close (2:30–4:00 PM)**

   ◦   Institutional money positions for
       overnight risk and next-day bias.

   ◦   Volatility spikes around 3:30 PM as
       funds finalize allocations.

   ◦   Clean reversals or acceleration moves
       often appear here — but they're
       continuations of setups mapped earlier
       in the day, not random shots in the
       dark.

Event-Driven Time Windows

Beyond daily cycles, **scheduled catalysts** create
predictable liquidity surges:

•   Economic reports (CPI, NFP, FOMC statements)

•   Earnings releases and guidance calls

•   Option expiration days (especially monthly and
    quarterly)

•   Federal Reserve announcements

- Geopolitical press briefings

Professionals **don't just know the calendar** — they know exactly *how the market tends to react in the 5–15 minutes before and after* each event, and they adjust size, stop placement, and aggression accordingly.

The Professional's Clock Mindset

You have to stop thinking about the market as "always on" and start thinking in **targeted hunting windows**:

- **Hunt when volatility and liquidity converge.**

- **Stand down when the prey is sleeping.**

- Use the quiet windows for **mapping, journaling, and planning**, not for revenge-trading or boredom trades.

Case Study: How Timing Saves Capital

Imagine two traders both short the same rejection pattern.

- Trader A enters at 10:05 AM — during opening volatility — and captures the flush for 3R.

- Trader B enters the *same pattern* at 12:15 PM — during midday chop — and gets stopped out as price grinds sideways and spikes back.

The pattern was identical. The **time was the difference** between profit and loss.

Building Your Time Discipline

- **Define your A+ windows** — for most day traders, that's the first 45–90 minutes and the last 60–90 minutes of the day.

- **Have a shutdown time** — if nothing's there by your cutoff, you're done.

- **Track your P/L by time of day** — you'll quickly see your own internal "sweet spots" where you make money consistently.

The Psychological Edge of Timing Mastery

When you know when to hunt and when to stand down:

- You feel less *FOMO* because you understand the clock is part of the edge.

- You stop bleeding slow losses in dead zones.

- You learn to compress your focus into high-probability hours — and your energy stays sharper for the trades that matter.

Professionals don't trade more; they trade **when it's worth it**.

Chapter 13 — Capital Warfare: How Professionals Deploy and Protect Money

Why Capital is Ammunition, Not Just Balance

For an amateur, the account balance is a scoreboard.
For a professional, **capital is ammunition** — finite, strategic, and never deployed recklessly. Every trade is a military engagement. You don't fire unless the conditions justify the risk.

The market is not about "making money" every day — it's about *surviving long enough* for the high-probability moments to arrive. The trader who runs out of ammo before the real battle begins is already dead.

Capital Preservation is Offensive Strategy

A common retail misconception: "Protecting capital" means being defensive or passive. In reality, preservation **is** the offense — it ensures you're fully armed when the rare, asymmetric opportunity emerges.

Capital is not for "practice."
Capital is for *deployment when conditions are ideal*. If the market is giving mixed signals, you're in the weeds — not in battle. Professionals *don't fire in the weeds*.

Risk Per Trade is Non-Negotiable

The pro's mindset:

- If a trade setup cannot justify the defined risk, it's not a trade.

- Position size is calculated backward from risk, not forward from greed.

- The **worst possible move** is increasing size on a lower-quality setup "just to make it worth it."

Amateurs trade to *feel in the game*. Pros trade to *extract capital from the market without jeopardizing survival*.

Deployment Models

1. **Fixed-Risk Model**

   - Same % or $ risk per trade regardless of conviction.

   - Pros use this early in a career or during a cold streak to maintain consistency and reduce mental variance.

2. **Tiered Conviction Model**

   - Low, medium, and high-conviction risk tiers.

   - Size expands only when multiple conditions align — market context, liquidity location, and personal readiness.

3. **Scaling-In with Control**

   - Adds are planned *before* entry, not improvised in panic.

   - Only added into when the trade thesis is *proven*, not as a "hope" rescue.

The Kill Shot Mindset

In elite capital warfare, you may fire 10–15 "probing shots" a month — small risk, testing the market's temperature — but when the kill shot emerges, you unload maximum allowable size.

The kill shot:

- Happens in ideal market conditions

- Aligns with your highest-probability pattern

- Occurs in your A+ time window

- Offers asymmetric reward to risk

- Has minimal conflicting data

If you risk 0.5% on probes, you may risk 3–5% on the kill shot.
This is where the bulk of annual P/L is made — **not in the noise, but in the moments that matter**.

Capital Drain Awareness

Professionals monitor their *capital bleed rate* like a general tracking troop losses. If you're leaking 5–10% a month in chop, you'll never be positioned to capitalize on the real move.

Signs you're bleeding capital unnecessarily:

- Trading outside your A+ windows

- Trading setups that are "kinda there"

- Adding to losers without hard invalidation

- Overtrading slow sessions out of boredom

Cash as a Strategic Weapon

There is a mental shift when you realize that **cash is a position**:

- If the market is untradeable, being in cash is equivalent to holding your army back from an unwinnable battle.

- When you see the perfect setup, you can then strike with full strength — *because you haven't been bleeding in the meantime.*

The Institutional Layer

Institutions don't just think in terms of account size — they think in *drawdown tolerance* and *return on deployed capital*.

- They can run months at breakeven if that means they avoid major drawdowns.

- They don't measure success by "green days," but by **preserving capital until the liquidity environment turns favorable**.

Action Protocol

To operate like a professional in capital warfare:

1. **Set absolute daily and weekly loss limits** — you stop trading when they're hit.

2. **Know your capital bleed rate** — how much you lose in non-ideal conditions.

3.   **Scale size according to conviction and
     environment**, not emotion.

4.   **Preserve ammunition** until the kill shot — resist
     the urge to fight in bad terrain.

Capital is your survival. Lose it carelessly, and you're out
of the war before the real battles begin.

Chapter 14 — The Execution Environment: Engineering Your Trading War Room

Why Environment Dictates Execution

Every trader likes to believe success is all about strategy and psychology — but the *environment* you trade in either amplifies or sabotages both. The professional treats their trading environment as a **military-grade operations center**.

An elite war room is designed to:

- Minimize noise — physical, mental, and informational

- Maximize decision speed and clarity

- Maintain your *state* in optimal performance mode for hours

- Remove any source of cognitive drag

If you've ever made an impulsive trade because of distraction, slow data, or poor setup — you've experienced the cost of an unoptimized environment.

Physical Environment — The Foundation

1. **Ergonomics and Physical Comfort**

   ○ You can't operate at your best if you're physically uncomfortable.

- Desk height, monitor placement, and chair support all directly impact how long you can remain in peak focus without fatigue.

- Pros use chairs designed for pilots, operators, or competitive gamers — not generic office furniture.

2. **Screens & Visual Real Estate**

- Multiple monitors aren't for "looking cool."

- The point is **information segmentation** — each screen has a defined role (execution, scanning, order flow, news, journaling).

- Cluttered, overlapping windows create missed opportunities and mental friction.

3. **Lighting & Visual Fatigue**

- The pros use adjustable lighting that matches screen brightness to avoid eye strain.

- Natural light boosts alertness — but avoid glare on screens.

4. **The Zero-Clutter Rule**

- Anything on your desk that is not directly contributing to trading performance is a liability.

- Your workspace should signal to your brain: *This is the battlefield.*

Digital Environment — The Silent Killer

1. **Information Overload**

   ○ Most retail traders drown in indicators, news feeds, and chatrooms.

   ○ Professionals cut **everything non-essential**. Your chart should only show what is absolutely required for *your* process.

2. **Platform Stability & Speed**

   ○ Lag, order execution errors, or data delays are unacceptable.

   ○ If your platform freezes once a week, you're operating at amateur level.

   ○ Pros test execution speed in both normal and high-volatility conditions.

3. **Distraction Management**

   ○ Email notifications, pop-ups, and phone alerts are execution poison.

   ○ In your trading window, you should be unreachable unless the building is on fire.

4. **Trading Journal Integration**

   ○ The journal should be *in your environment*, not something you "do later."

   ○ Professionals integrate post-trade notes within minutes, not hours, to capture emotional state and reasoning while it's fresh.

Mental Environment — The Invisible Edge

1. State Priming

- Before the market opens, pros enter a *performance state*.

- This can be as simple as a 10-minute visualization of market scenarios and execution responses.

- The goal: walk into the open with mental readiness, not emotional noise.

2. Energy Management

- Trading burns cognitive fuel faster than most professions.

- Elite traders schedule breaks at precise intervals to reset mental clarity before it degrades.

- Nutrition and hydration are treated as operational requirements, not afterthoughts.

3. Stress Containment

- Even pros feel stress — the difference is they contain it within **predefined protocols**.

- For example: two losing trades in a row → mandatory 20-minute reset away from screens.

War Room Protocols

1. **Start-of-Day Scan** — Review overnight market developments, key levels, and plan for the session.

2. **Market Open Phase** — Focus on A+ setups only, ignore all "maybe" trades.

3. **Mid-Session Review** — Quick check-in on execution quality and emotional state.

4. **Closing Procedures** — Flatten positions, log trades, mark charts, review performance.

5. **Post-Market Debrief** — Identify one improvement for the next session.

The Professional Reality

Your environment is either **compounding focus or compounding mistakes**.
The difference between a trader who executes flawlessly and one who self-sabotages often comes down to physical, digital, and mental space — not strategy.

If your workspace feels casual, your execution will be casual. If your war room feels like the cockpit of a fighter jet, your brain will adapt to operate like a pilot.

Chapter 15 — The Operator's Console: Execution Technology & Tools of the Professional

Why Tools Decide Survival

Strategy is useless if your tools can't execute it. The market is a latency war, a visibility war, and a routing war. Pros don't guess with mouse clicks on retail platforms. They engineer their console so every decision has a direct, frictionless pipeline into the tape. If your hardware, software, and order routing are sloppy, you've already donated before you click.

Your edge is not only *what you see* — it's *how fast you can act on what you see, and how invisible you remain while doing it.*

1. The Screen Architecture

Amateurs pile everything on one monitor, tabbing between charts like tourists in traffic. Pros build **segmented visual architecture**:

- **Primary Execution Screen** — 1–2 instruments you trade actively. No clutter. Just clean order book, tape, VWAP, key anchors.

- **Context Screen** — Index futures, correlated sectors, vol indices. This prevents tunnel vision.

- **Liquidity/Flow Screen** — Volume profile, options OI heatmap, imbalance trackers. This is your battlefield map.

- **News/Feed Screen** — Only curated institutional feeds (not Twitter noise). You want timestamps and speed, not commentary.

- **Journal/Process Screen** — Immediate access to notes, screenshots, trade logs. Reflection is part of execution, not afterthought.

The architecture must be consistent. Same positions every day. Cognitive friction kills milliseconds.

2. Order Types: The Hidden Weaponry

Retail sees "limit" and "market." Pros know there's an arsenal underneath:

- **Iceberg / Reserve Orders** — Show 100 shares, hide 9,900. Essential for sponsors unloading without flashing size.

- **Midpoint Pegs** — Execute between bid/ask. Quiet fills, stealth accumulation.

- **Hide-Not-Slide** — Stay hidden even when price shifts through your order. Avoids giving away intent.

- **Discretionary Pegs** — Resting order with small range of discretion; captures liquidity without chasing.

- **Conditional Orders** — Trigger only if conditions met (VWAP touch, stop-through). Pre-loads discipline.

If you're not fluent in these order types, you're fighting the market with a toy knife while pros wield scalpels.

3. Routing & Venues: Where Your Order Actually Lands

Your broker is not neutral. Every route is a choice of battlefield:

- **Lit Exchanges (NYSE, NASDAQ):** Visible, but you're the prey. Breakouts die because liquidity already printed dark before you saw it.

- **Dark Pools / ATS:** Hidden venues where size trades without alerting lit tape. If you don't account for them, you'll misread why a "perfect" level failed.

- **Internalizers / Wholesalers:** Most retail orders never touch the exchange. They're matched internally against other flow. If you don't know this, you can't see the true battlefield.

Pro move: Route selectively. Use lit only when you want to *signal* strength. Hide size where you don't want the tape chasing you. Execution is theater as much as mechanics.

4. Speed & Latency: The Invisible Edge

Milliseconds matter. Every delay compounds slippage:

- **Hardware:** Pros don't run multi-million dollar decisions on laptops with browser tabs open. Dedicated machine, max RAM, low-latency network card.

- **Network:** Hard-wired fiber, backup ISP, UPS power protection. A Wi-Fi drop during execution is career-ending.

- **Platform Stability:** If your chart freezes once a week, you're amateur. Pros stress-test in high-volatility conditions before real size.

Latency is not only speed of entry — it's speed of *awareness*. The sooner you see imbalance prints or hidden absorption, the earlier you survive.

5. Tape & Flow Reading Tools

The screen is the shadow. The tape is the bloodstream.

- **Time & Sales (T&S):** Raw prints reveal intent faster than candles. Look for repetitive sizes, hidden icebergs, or vacuum bursts.

- **Order Book / Level 2:** Most size is spoof, but watching how bids/offers reload or vanish tells you sponsor intent.

- **Volume Profile & VWAP Anchors:** Where business was actually done, not just where price touched. These are the gravity points.

- **Options Flow Trackers:** Unusual block prints or OI shifts often reveal sponsor hedging pressure.

Tape reading is not nostalgia — it's the only way to see sponsor intent before the chart confirms it.

6. Automation Without Abdication

Algos aren't enemies — they're force multipliers if controlled.

- **Execution Algos (TWAP/VWAP):** Sponsors use them to mask size. You can shadow their footprints.

- **Conditional Bracket Orders:** Auto-place stops/ targets instantly on entry. Removes emotional hesitation.

- **Alerts & Scripting:** Automate the boring — VWAP reclaims, profile alerts, liquidity vacuum entries. But never abdicate decision-making to a bot. Automation is assistant, not commander.

7. Building Your Operator's Console

A professional console isn't expensive toys. It's **clarity, speed, and stealth**:

- Strip every chart to essentials — VWAP, profile, liquidity anchors.

- Hotkeys for instant entries/exits.

- Multiple routes available, chosen with intent.

- Tape, profile, options flow visible at all times.

- Journal integrated live.

If your console doesn't feel like a cockpit — consistent, stripped, lethal — you're not operating at pro standard.

Operator's Commandments of Technology

1. **Every extra click is a tax.** Reduce friction or lose fills.

2. **Every visible order is information leaked.** Show only what you intend.

3. **Every freeze or lag is sabotage.** Test, upgrade, or quit.

4. **Your console is your cockpit.** Treat it like life support, not a gaming setup.

5. **Tools don't make you pro.** But without pro tools, you'll never survive long enough to become one.

The console is not optional equipment; it is risk management in disguise. Every pro builds it to enforce three non-negotiables: first, orders must fire without delay — meaning hotkeys mapped, brackets pre-loaded, and backup routes tested daily. Second, information must stay hidden — reserve orders, midpoint pegs, and selective dark routing should be second nature, not exotic tools. Third, the layout must reduce decisions, not multiply them — execution screen, context screen, flow screen, nothing else. If these conditions are not locked, then every trade you take carries hidden slippage, exposure, and hesitation that a sponsor can exploit. The architecture of your console is the architecture of your survival.

Chapter 16 — The Professional Trader's Code: Non-Negotiables That Separate the Few from the Many

There's a quiet, unspoken code among traders who have made it past the threshold where survival is no longer in question.

It's not written in beginner books. It's not discussed in chatrooms. You learn it either by paying for it in losses, or by being around people who already live it.

This chapter is that code.
These are not tips, preferences, or "best practices."
These are **laws**. Violate them, and you will eventually pay in capital, confidence, or your career.

Law 1 — Protect Capital as If It's Oxygen

Professionals don't think of capital as money — they think of it as *breathing capacity*.

Every bad trade that violates risk parameters isn't just a loss, it's a reduction in the number of breaths you have left before suffocation.

If you lose too much oxygen too quickly, you don't have time to make the right decisions when the market finally gives you an opening.

The pro knows: **capital preserved is opportunity preserved**.

Law 2 — One Career-Ending Mistake Is Always Lurking

The day you believe "that could never happen to me" is the day the market is about to test that belief.

Every professional operates with the constant awareness that a single uncontrolled position, a single moment of ego-driven stubbornness, can end years of work.

Institutional desks survive because they have built-in kill switches and enforce them ruthlessly.
A pro trader enforces their own kill switches with the same ruthlessness.

Law 3 — The Market Owes You Nothing

It doesn't owe you a green day.
It doesn't care that you "deserve" to make money after a losing week.
It doesn't reward effort — it only rewards alignment.

The amateur sees the market as a source of fairness or payback. The professional sees it as a **neutral battlefield** where advantage exists only for a moment and disappears without apology.

Law 4 — Risk Small, Scale Big Only When Earned

Pros start positions at size levels that don't threaten their mental stability.
Size is increased only when the trader is in sync with the market and the conditions justify it — not because "I feel confident today."

The code is simple:

- New or uncertain environment → smallest size.

- Clear, high-quality setup + mental alignment → scale.

Law 5 — Every Trade Has an Expiration Date

The market conditions that make a trade valid decay over time.
Amateurs get trapped because they cling to positions whose reason for existence has already died.
Pros have zero emotional investment once the original conditions are gone. They cut it, even if it means a small loss after hours of patience.

Law 6 — Personal Life = Trading Life

Your trading performance is a mirror of your personal operating system.
If you live in chaos — poor sleep, bad diet, constant distractions — your execution will reflect it.

Pros guard their lifestyle inputs like they guard their watchlist.
Energy, clarity, and discipline are not "trading skills" — they're consequences of how you run your entire life.

Law 7 — Never Let a Loss Teach You the Same Lesson Twice

Losing money is tuition. Paying the same tuition twice means you didn't learn.
Pros document, dissect, and correct — then they run systems to make the same mistake mechanically impossible to repeat.

Law 8 — The Trade Is Over When the Plan Is Over

The trade plan is your contract with yourself.
Once it's fulfilled — win or lose — the professional doesn't renegotiate.

Amateurs justify overstaying. Pros exit clean and move on.

Law 9 — Your Ego Is the Counterparty

In every major drawdown story, the counterparty wasn't the market — it was the trader's ego.
Pros know that every time they override a stop, revenge trade, or try to "show the market," they're not fighting the tape — they're fighting their own reflection.

Law 10 — Flat Is a Position

Amateurs believe they must always be in something.
Pros know that being flat is often the most profitable state possible because it preserves mental capital for when opportunity is undeniable.

Law 11 — Information Without Filtration Is Poison

You can drown in news, opinions, indicators, and social media chatter.
Pros filter inputs down to **only** what feeds their specific execution model.
Everything else is noise, and noise kills clarity.

Law 12 — Self-Audit Without Mercy

After the close, the professional rips apart their own execution without excuse.
They don't protect their feelings. They don't sugarcoat.
They identify the real cause — psychological, procedural, or structural — and fix it before the next open.

Law 13 — Survival > Heroics

There are no medals for biggest single-day gain.
The pros you never hear about are the ones who quietly

survive and grow year after year, while flashy "heroes" blow up accounts and disappear.

Survival is the real game. Heroics are ego traps.

These laws aren't optional. They form the **invisible guardrails** around every action an elite trader takes. They're why pros last for decades while others burn out in months.

Chapter 17 — The Performance Tracking Framework: Turning Discipline Into Data

If the Pro Code is the law, this chapter is the enforcement mechanism. Most traders journal like it's a diary: "I felt anxious. I should've been more patient. I'll do better tomorrow." That's not professional journaling — that's therapy. A professional journal is a black box flight recorder. It captures every decision, every input, and every output in a way that can be audited.

If you want to evolve into institutional grade, you need more than self-talk. You need a framework that turns discipline into metrics. You need to measure if you are trading like capital or like a person.

I. The Three Pillars of a Professional Journal

Every elite desk's P&L report combines three layers:

1.   **Expectancy Tracking** — Are your setups mathematically worth trading?

2.   **Temporal Edge Tracking** — Are you trading at the right times of day?

3.   **Flow Read Accuracy** — Are you correctly identifying the active sponsor?

Without all three, you're running blind.

II. Expectancy Tracking (The Real Edge Metric)

Every system boils down to expectancy:

$$E=(Win\% \times AvgWin -(Loss\% \times AvgLoss)$$

But retail misuses expectancy by treating it as one lump.
Pros disaggregate it:

- By **setup type** (VWAP reclaim, supply/demand, overnight trap, liquidity flush, etc.)

- By **market condition** (trend day, range day, news day)

- By **sponsor context** (dealer gamma, CTA flows, corporate buybacks)

Professional Application:

- Tag every trade with its setup archetype.

- Review quarterly: cut the bottom 20% setups, double down on the top 20%.

- This is how desks scale edge — not by "more trades," but by culling weak DNA.

III. Temporal Edge Tracking (The Clock Audit)

Most retail blow-ups happen because they trade the wrong
hours. You must track P&L by time of day:

- **Opening Drive (9:30–10:15)**

- **Post-Open Trend Test (10:15–11:30)**

- **Midday Drift (11:30–1:30)**

- **Power Hour (2:30–4:00)**

Professional Application:

- Journal *time of entry* and *time of exit*.

- Run rolling stats: which windows are net positive for you? Which bleed capital?

- The moment you see midday trades are consistently negative, you stop trading midday. No excuses.

The pro knows: one hour can carry the month — and another can erase it.

IV. Flow Read Accuracy (Were You Right About the Room?)

Execution without context is gambling. Your journal must track whether your sponsor read was correct, not just whether the trade won.

Each day, before entry, log:

- **Who is urgent today?** (Dealer? CTA? Corporate? Long-only?)

- **What clock is running?** (OpEx? rebalance? close? earnings window?)

- **What fuel is in play?** (stops above highs, LVN gap, VWAP reclaim?)

At the end of the session:

- Were you correct about the active archetype?

- If wrong, did you lose because of misread context or poor execution?

Over time, you build a hit rate for your *flow reads*. A trader with 70% flow-read accuracy but 50% trade win rate is closer to professional than someone with 70% win rate but zero idea who moved price.

V. P&L Architecture (Beyond Dollars)

Professional P&L is segmented:

1.   **Trade Risk Unit (TRU)** — fixed percentage of
      capital per trade (e.g., 0.5%).

2.   **Session Risk Unit (SRU)** — max allowable loss
      for the session (e.g., 2–3 TRU).

3.   **Monthly Risk Budget (MRB)** — total ammo for
      the month.

Your journal must log not just $ wins/losses, but % of TRU
and SRU consumed. This forces you to see whether you
survived the day within budget — or blew risk discipline
even if you "made money."

VI. The Performance Dashboard

By the end of each week, your dashboard should show:

•   **Setup Expectancy:** Which plays are paying,
     which are bleeding.

•   **Time-of-Day Edge:** Your "hot zones" and "death
     zones."

•   **Flow Read Accuracy:** Sponsor map hit rate.

•   **Risk Discipline:** % of days you stayed within
     TRU/SRU/MRB.

This is your scoreboard. Not P&L alone — but alignment
with professional process.

VII. The Professional Review Loop

Pros don't just journal. They review systematically:

- **Daily:** Quick log, note edge adherence.

- **Weekly:** Pull stats, highlight strongest and weakest edges.

- **Monthly:** Adjust size, cull weak setups, refine watchlist.

- **Quarterly:** Rewrite playbook rules based on data.

Retail journals collect dust. Pro journals evolve the trader.

VIII. Why This Changes Everything

With this framework, you are no longer asking:

- "Am I good enough?"

- "Do I feel disciplined today?"

- "Is this the right setup?"

Instead, you know:

- Which setups pay.

- Which hours bleed.

- Whether your flow reads are accurate.

- Whether you are trading inside professional constraints.

This turns trading from a subjective rollercoaster into an institutional feedback loop. It is the difference between "a guy with a journal" and "a desk with a risk manager."

Chapter 18 — The Mental Weaponry of the Elite: Tools, Triggers, and Tactical Mindshifts Used in Live Combat

Trading at the highest level is not just a test of analysis or execution — it's an arena where your own mind can either be your most dangerous enemy or your most powerful weapon.
The difference between those two outcomes is **what mental tools you have at hand in the heat of battle**.

The market moves too fast for you to "try to be calm" or "remind yourself to focus." That's kindergarten advice.
The elite operate with **trained reflexive triggers** — systems of thought and perception that fire automatically when conditions demand it.

This chapter is about those weapons.
They're not affirmations. They're not motivational quotes.
They're **combat tools** — built for the chaos of a live market where milliseconds matter.

Weapon 1 — The Pre-Loaded Decision Stack

When elite traders enter a session, they've already reduced their potential decision tree for every scenario they might face.
They don't "figure it out in the moment." They've **pre-committed** to specific responses if X, Y, or Z happens.

Example:

- If price approaches VWAP with rising volume and inside my high-probability time window → I already know my entry size, my stop, and my exit target range.

- If the opposite happens, I already know I'm flat — no debate, no hesitation.

Why it matters: In live combat, hesitation costs fills, good prices, and mental energy. The decision stack removes hesitation entirely.

Weapon 2 — Emotional Interrupt Switch

Every pro has an internal "circuit breaker" to interrupt an emotional spiral before it hits execution.
This is not "take a deep breath" — this is an *instant pattern disruptor*.

It might be:

- Standing up and walking away for 90 seconds mid-trade (yes, even with money on the line) to break fixation.

- A pre-set audio cue that you trigger when you feel FOMO or frustration rising.

- Physically moving your mouse hand off the desk when you recognize revenge-trade impulses.

Why it matters: You can't think your way out of a spiral once you're in it — you have to *break state* instantly.

Weapon 3 — Context Lock

The elite never lose sight of the higher frame while working the micro frame.
They lock their context before the open — what's the overall market regime? Is today a mean-reversion or trend day?
Once locked, they don't allow noise from a single candle or a random news headline to pull them out of that frame.

Why it matters: Most traders get chopped because they switch bias 15 times a day based on meaningless short-term moves. Context lock prevents that drift.

Weapon 4 — The Two-Tier Risk View

Pro traders don't just think in "dollars at risk" — they think in **structural risk** and **psychological risk** simultaneously.

- Structural: Does this trade fit within my overall risk framework?

- Psychological: If this loses, will it pull me off-center for the next trade?

If the psychological risk is too high, they pass — even if the trade looks "good."

Why it matters: A single emotionally damaging loss can ruin the rest of your day more than the dollars lost.

Weapon 5 — The Silent Countdown

Many pros use time as a mental anchor.
When volatility spikes, they'll silently count (5… 4… 3… 2… 1…) before executing or cutting a trade.

This 3–5 second pause:

- Clears the adrenaline spike.

- Gives your prefrontal cortex time to override the fight-or-flight impulse.

- Allows you to re-check the plan before committing.

Why it matters: In high-speed markets, your instinctive brain will always try to front-run your rational brain. The countdown reverses that.

Weapon 6 — The Posture Reset

When things go off track, elite traders reset physically before they reset mentally.
This could mean:

- Adjusting their seat height to change eye level on the screens.

- Re-aligning monitors so their focus is directly on the primary chart.

- Even moving to a standing position if seated losses start stacking.

Why it matters: Physical position influences perception. A simple posture shift can flip your mental state faster than self-talk.

Weapon 7 — Mental Auto-Scaling

In live conditions, the elite automatically scale back size if they detect any mental slippage — hesitation, overthinking, emotional spikes.
The size reduction is instantaneous and needs no debate.

Why it matters: Staying in the game is more important than proving a point with size. This reflex keeps capital and mental stability intact.

Weapon 8 — Detached Observation Mode

Every top trader knows how to slip into a mental state
where they watch the market like an outsider.
They imagine themselves as a hired analyst, **not** the trader
whose money is at risk.

Why it matters: The distance created in this mental mode
reduces attachment and allows for cleaner execution.

Weapon 9 — End-of-Day Amnesia

The elite have trained themselves to treat each day as
completely independent of the last.
Yesterday's P&L — win or loss — is irrelevant to today's
execution.

Why it matters: Most traders unconsciously anchor
today's confidence level to yesterday's results, sabotaging
both upswings and downswings.

These tools aren't theoretical — they are **operational edge
multipliers**.
Without them, all the setups and technical skill in the world
won't stop the market from draining you psychologically.

Chapter 19 — Failure Autopsy: Why 99% of Traders Die in the Arena

If the Performance Tracking Framework is about building your black box recorder, this chapter is the crash investigation. It is the morgue tour — the autopsy of the exact mistakes that bury traders.

Every failure is predictable. Every blow-up has a cause of death that could have been prevented. What ends careers is not bad luck, not "algos," not "manipulation" — it's the same four or five lethal errors repeated with different costumes.

This is the gallery of corpses. Read it, and you will never be able to say you weren't warned.

I. The Anatomy of a Trading Death

Most careers don't end in one bad trade — they end in **stacked violations**:

- Ignoring phase context.

- Ignoring capital limits.

- Ignoring calendar gravity.

- Ignoring their own tilt signals.
  Each by itself is survivable. Stack them together, and it's terminal.

The law of professional survival: **You can only survive if you never let failures compound.**

II. Failure Mode #1: Over-Leverage (Death by Size)

Cause of Death: Position size exceeds psychological and capital capacity.

- The trader risks 10–20% of capital on a single trade.

- When wrong, they freeze, refuse to cut, and spiral into revenge adds.

- Even if "it works once," it hardwires a death habit.

Case Study — The Widowmaker:
Retail trader sizes into Tesla earnings at 8x normal risk. Trade gaps 12% against. Account is down 70% overnight. The career is over.

Autopsy Note:
You can survive being wrong. You cannot survive betting your oxygen tank.

III. Failure Mode #2: Tilt Loops (Death by Emotion)

Cause of Death: Losing control after a loss and compounding errors.

- Revenge trading after a stop-out.

- Doubling size to "make it back."

- Trading outside normal windows because of FOMO.

Case Study — The Afternoon Spiral:
Trader takes a 0.5% hit in the open. Gets emotional. Trades midday chop, loses another 1%. At 3:30 PM, doubles size

in desperation. Loses 5%. One small loss turned into career damage.

Autopsy Note:
Tilt doesn't just kill capital — it kills your future edge by rewiring your brain into desperation mode.

IV. Failure Mode #3: Phase Ignorance (Death by Context Blindness)

Cause of Death: Trading as if every candle has equal meaning, ignoring daily phases and sponsor objectives.

- Chasing the open drive when it's engineered trap.

- Fighting the midday drift as if it were momentum.

- Treating the close as final truth instead of sponsor staging.

Case Study — The Open Drive Victim:
Trader sees breakout at 9:37 AM, piles in size. Stops out in 2 minutes as sponsor reverses. Keeps re-entering all morning. Never realized the "move" was sponsor inventory alignment.

Autopsy Note:
Every day is segmented. If you don't know the phase, you are fighting a ghost.

V. Failure Mode #4: Calendar Amnesia (Death by Time)

Cause of Death: Forgetting that time moves money.

- Ignoring OpEx pin risk.

- Trading breakouts into FOMC announcements.

- Holding risk into rebalance closes without awareness.

Case Study — The Fed Victim:
Trader is long breakout at 1:55 PM on FOMC day. Rates release at 2:00. Position gets obliterated in the whipsaw. Loss wipes two months of gains.

Autopsy Note:
The calendar is not background noise. It is half the market. Forget it, and you're trading blindfolded into a minefield.

VI. Failure Mode #5: Narrative Addiction (Death by Story)

Cause of Death: Believing the story more than the tape.

- "AI is the future — this breakout is real."

- "The Fed is dovish — this dip can't last."

- "This stock is undervalued — it must go up."

Case Study — The Bagholder:
Trader buys into euphoric headline at distribution phase. Holds through absorption. Refuses to cut because "the story is right." Position drifts, then collapses. Career dies with it.

Autopsy Note:
The story exists to serve sponsor exits. If you are trading the story, you are the liquidity.

VII. Failure Mode #6: Over-Trading (Death by a Thousand Cuts)

Cause of Death: Bleeding out slowly through low-quality trades.

- Trading every wiggle.

- Refusing to wait for A+ setups.

- Believing activity = progress.

Case Study — The Scalper Corpse:
Trader takes 40 trades in a day. Wins 20, loses 20. Commission, slippage, and mental fatigue erase all gains. Account bleeds out over months.

Autopsy Note:
Activity feeds brokers, not your account. Discipline is the rarest commodity.

VIII. Failure Mode #7: Ego Override (Death by Identity)

Cause of Death: Refusing to accept being wrong.

- Moving stops "to give it room."

- Holding losers because "I can't take another red day."

- Doubling down to prove a point.

Case Study — The Blow-Up Hero:
Trader short squeezes, refuses to cut. Keeps adding. Gets margin-called at the highs. Account wiped. Still insists: "I was right — the market was wrong."

Autopsy Note:
The market has no memory. Your ego does. That's why it kills you.

IX. The Unified Cause of Death

When you examine enough corpses, the truth is clear:

- **Over-Leverage** fuels the fatal wound.

- **Tilt** accelerates blood loss.

- **Phase Ignorance** and **Calendar Amnesia** blindfold the victim.

- **Narrative Addiction** keeps them in denial.

- **Over-Trading** drains them slowly.

- **Ego** prevents the stop-loss that could have saved them.

Every obituary reads differently. Every cause of death is the same.

X. The Autopsy Oath

Pin this above your screens:

- I will never risk my oxygen tank.

- I will kill tilt after the first sign, not after the third loss.

- I will map phase and calendar before trading any candle.

- I will never trade the story — only the flow.

- I will treat activity as a cost, not as proof of discipline.

- I will cut ego at the throat before it cuts my account.

Every failure mode is just a different mask on the same truth: the market kills hesitation, ego, and ignorance with perfect efficiency. Sponsors don't need to beat you — they only need you to step outside discipline once. The moment you forget the phase, oversize your trade, ignore the calendar, or chase a headline, you've already written your own obituary. This is why the professional operates with merciless rules: not because rules feel safe, but because without them you are unarmed in a battlefield designed to exploit every lapse. The graveyard is full of talent. The only traders who survive are the ones who enforce rules without exception.

Chapter 20 — The Tactical Day Structure of a Pro: How Elite Traders Dominate Every Segment of the Session

Most traders think the market is one continuous stream of opportunity from bell to bell.
Pros know it's not.
The day has **natural rhythms, energy spikes, and probability zones** — and each demands a different mental and tactical stance.

If you treat 9:30 a.m. like 1:45 p.m., you're already trading at a disadvantage.
This chapter is about **structuring your day like an elite operator** so you're in peak execution mode exactly when the market is offering its best.

Segment 1 — The Pre-Market War Room (6:00 a.m.– 9:29 a.m. ET)

This is not "sip coffee and check Twitter" time.
This is the **war room** — the mental and informational pre-load that sets the entire tone for your day.

Objectives:

1. **Define the Battlefield** — Understand the overnight session, futures movement, major news catalysts, and the macro bias for the day.

2. **Lock Your Playbook** — Decide your 1–3 core trade ideas or scenarios. Not 10. Not "see what happens."

3.   **Rehearse the Triggers** — Visualize exactly what a green-light trade looks like today. This is the mental equivalent of dry-firing a weapon before a mission.

4.   **Set the Mental Guardrails** — Decide your maximum loss limit, your cutoff time for trading if you're not in sync, and any behavioral rules specific to today's conditions.

Pro Mindset Here:
The pre-market isn't about finding trades — it's about *killing all the trades you're not going to take*.
Clarity is a weapon.

Segment 2 — The Opening Shockwave (9:30 a.m.–10:00 a.m.)

This is the **most dangerous and most lucrative window** of the day.
Volume and volatility are at their peak, spreads can widen, and algos are in full hunt mode.

Objectives:

1.   **Observe First, Strike Second** — Unless you are specifically trained for open-drive setups, let the first few minutes reveal order flow.

2.   **Identify the Control Zones** — See where price repeatedly rejects or accepts — these are the opening battle lines.

3.   **Execute with Pre-Loaded Triggers** — Only fire trades that match the exact playbook rehearsed in pre-market.

Pro Mindset Here:
If you can't read the open, the rest of the day will often be a blur.
The elite either make their day here or they let the market tip its hand before engaging.

Segment 3 — The Post-Open Trend Test (10:00 a.m.–11:30 a.m.)

By now, the initial liquidity burst has calmed, and the **true directional bias** for the morning is more visible.

Objectives:

1. **Confirm or Reject the Morning Bias** — Is the trend from the open holding or failing?

2. **Look for First Pullback Entries** — This is prime time for pullback trades into established momentum.

3. **Avoid Over-Trading the Noise** — If the market is choppy, reduce size or sit out.

Pro Mindset Here:
This is where many amateurs give back their opening gains — by forcing trades in dead zones.
Pros extract the meat and step back when the tape says "low probability."

Segment 4 — The Midday Grind (11:30 a.m.–1:30 p.m.)

This is **where capital is destroyed** by boredom.
Liquidity is thin, algos control more of the flow, and emotional fatigue starts creeping in.

Objectives:

1. **Preserve Mental and Financial Capital** — This is often "defense mode" unless a major news catalyst drops.

2. **Review the Morning** — If you're green, consider locking the day. If you're red, this is not the time to "make it back."

3. **Research or Prep for Power Hour** — Use the lull to refine watchlists or spot late-day positioning.

Pro Mindset Here:

The elite know when *not* to fight. This period is often a reset — not a hunting ground.

Segment 5 — The Power Hour Setup Window (1:30 p.m.–3:00 p.m.)

Liquidity begins to build again. Institutions start positioning for the close.
This is a **secondary prime time** — but it requires a different lens than the morning.

Objectives:

1. **Identify the Dominant Afternoon Narrative** — Is the market continuing the morning trend or reversing it?

2. **Look for Trapped Traders** — Late shorts or longs from midday who are now being squeezed.

3. **Use Time as a Weapon** — Afternoon trades need tighter timing — you have less runway before the bell.

Pro Mindset Here:
If you missed the morning, this is your second chance —
but execution must be precise and lean.

Segment 6 — The Closing Drive (3:00 p.m.–4:00 p.m.)

The final hour is about **order imbalances, window
dressing, and liquidation**.
It can be explosive — or a controlled drift.

Objectives:

1. **Exploit End-of-Day Positioning** — Fade
exhausted moves or ride late surges with
conviction.

2. **Close the Book** — Finish the day clean — no
"Hail Mary" trades that undo hours of discipline.

3. **Do the Post-Mortem** — Journal your key
decisions, your emotional state, and what you'll
adjust tomorrow.

Pro Mindset Here:
Elite traders finish with **intentionality**. The last trade of the
day is never random.

Why This Structure Works

- **Protects Focus** — You are only fully "on" when
probability is on your side.

- **Matches Energy to Opportunity** — You avoid
wasting mental stamina in low-probability zones.

- **Reduces Emotional Tilt** — Each segment has its
own rules and mindset, so you don't drag
mistakes forward.

Chapter 21 — The Psychology of Capital Preservation: How Elite Traders Stay in the Game for Decades

If there's one truth that separates the elite from the endless graveyard of traders who flame out, it's this:

The market doesn't reward the smartest. It rewards the ones still alive when the rare, asymmetric opportunity arrives.

Preservation is not about being timid. It's about understanding that **capital is not just money — it is time, optionality, and psychological firepower**. When you blow up, you don't just lose dollars; you lose *time in the arena* and the *mental edge* to act decisively when the real plays show up.

The Capital Mindset Shift

Most traders treat their account as a "scoreboard." They wake up looking to *win points* every day.
Pros treat their account as a **weapons cache** — one they protect with the paranoia of a soldier guarding the last ammo dump in a war zone.

- Every trade either **fortifies** that cache or **erodes** it.

- The goal is not to win today; it's to remain *fully armed* for tomorrow, next week, next year.

The 3 Dimensions of Capital Preservation

1. Financial Capital – The Obvious but Mismanaged Resource

This is the raw ammunition. Blow it, and the game ends instantly.

Elite Behaviors:

- **Hard Daily Loss Limits** — They never "give the market a second chance" to take more.

- **Scaled Sizing** — Risk per trade shrinks in low-quality conditions; it only expands when everything lines up.

- **Capital Deployment Windows** — They know the 10–15 sessions per month that are worth pushing size. The rest are for surgical trades or no trades at all.

2. Emotional Capital – The Silent Killer

Your psychological reserve is finite. Once it's drained, you start doing damage to both yourself and your account.

Elite Behaviors:

- **Cut Early When Off-Kilter** — They recognize mental tilt *before* it blows up into a losing streak.

- **Trade Count Limits** — Prevent decision fatigue by setting a max trades per session.

- **Recovery Protocols** — When emotional capital is low, they step back for a day or more without hesitation.

3. Reputational Capital – The Hidden Asset

If you aspire to trade other people's money or join institutional capital, your reputation *is* capital. Blow that, and you're radioactive.

Elite Behaviors:

* **No Revenge Trading in Public Accounts** — They know one reckless day can erase years of trust.

* **Consistent Process Over Flashy Wins** — They'd rather be boring and bankable than volatile and "exciting."

* **Aligned Incentives** — Never put themselves in positions where desperation forces bad trades.

The Core Rule of Survivorship

Your #1 job is to be in the chair, fully loaded, when the market finally gifts you the fat pitch.

That pitch might come twice a month. It might come twice a year.
If you're emotionally or financially crippled when it comes, you'll either miss it or lack the size to capitalize.

The Preservation Protocol

Start Each Month with an "Ammo Budget" — Allocate risk for the month in advance.
Think of this like a military campaign budget: you set aside the maximum you are willing to lose for the month before you even open the first trade.

- Example: If your risk capital is $50,000 and you allocate 5% per month, then your "ammo budget" is $2,500. Once it's spent, you're out of the game until the next month. This keeps you from death-by-a-thousand-cuts or blowing up in a cold streak.

Tag Each Day as Offensive or Defensive — Based on volatility, setups, and your own mental state.
Not every day is for attack. Some days are only for survival.

- Example: If it's FOMC day, volatility is high and your setups align, you tag it as **Offensive** — you're cleared to push size. If it's a slow summer Friday, or you wake up distracted and tired, you tag it as **Defensive** — size small or don't trade at all. Labeling the day before it starts keeps emotion out of the decision.

Track Energy, Not Just P&L — Journal your emotional state daily and monitor for erosion.
Capital isn't the only account you manage — your energy is finite too.

- Example: If you notice after three losing days that your notes say "frustrated, distracted, tired," your emotional capital is bleeding. Even if P&L looks fine, it's time to stand down or cut size until the energy account is recharged.

Have a Rapid Exit Plan for All Damage — If down big early, know exactly how you will shut it down.
Every professional has a kill switch. You don't wait until panic sets in — you know the rule beforehand.

- Example: "If I'm down 1.5R by 11:00 AM, I shut down for the day." This prevents tilt spirals and locks the loss before it metastasizes.

Audit Your Reputation Quarterly — Review your trading record and public footprint as if you were hiring yourself.

Your reputation *is* capital. Blow it, and you'll never manage OPM (other people's money).

- Example: Every quarter, review your track record: are your losses controlled, are your drawdowns shallow, is your process consistent? If you posted your stats publicly, would they attract investors — or scare them away? Treat your name like an asset under management.

Why Capital Preservation Feels Boring — and Why That's the Point

Amateurs crave action. They measure success by *activity*. Pros know boredom is a sign they're not bleeding out unnecessarily.

The goal isn't to trade every day — it's to trade **forever**.

Chapter 22 — The Execution Mind: Pulling the Trigger Like a Machine Without Losing the Human Edge

In the end, **trading is not about ideas — it's about execution**.

You can know everything about market structure, read the tape perfectly, and still end up with a flat or negative P&L if your execution is sloppy. Execution is the thin line between being right in theory and being right in your account statement.

Why Execution is the Final Bottleneck

There's a harsh truth:
Most traders are not limited by lack of knowledge; they're limited by their inability to act **with precision, speed, and conviction** when the time comes.

The market rewards those who can:

- Recognize opportunity instantly.

- Commit with the correct size.

- Manage the trade without emotional drift.

- Exit without hesitation when wrong.

Building the Execution Mind

Execution is a **trained reflex**, not a moment of inspiration. The more discretionary your trading style, the more dangerous it becomes if your execution reflex is weak.

The elite approach execution like this:

1. Pre-Decision Before the Session

- They decide before the market opens *what will qualify as an actionable trade*.

- They predefine size, stop, and target ranges.

- This means that during live action, the decision is 80% already made — the only question is "Did my conditions hit?"

2. Reducing Execution Friction

Every extra click, every manual adjustment is friction — and friction creates hesitation.

- **Hotkeys and Templates** — Orders are one keystroke away, preloaded with stops and targets.

- **Chart Cleanliness** — No visual clutter. The more visual noise, the slower the trigger pull.

- **Position Sizing Automation** — Size is calculated automatically based on stop distance, removing mental math under pressure.

3. Emotional Firewalling

When you pull the trigger, emotion must be **quarantined**. That doesn't mean you don't feel — it means you don't *act* on feeling mid-trade.

Pro tactics:

- **Execution Breathing** — One controlled breath before entry, one after — reduces adrenaline spikes.

- **Emotion Journaling** — Immediate notes on what you felt at entry; awareness reduces future repetition of bad habits.

- **Non-Overlapping Focus** — When in a trade, focus on managing it — not scanning for the next one.

4. Instant Loss Acceptance

Pros don't "hope" after entry. If the stop hits, they are out. Full stop.

- No re-entry unless *all* criteria reset.

- No moving stops further to "give it room."

- No "I'll just scale in until it turns" — that's not execution, that's gambling.

5. Exiting with Aggression When Wrong

Being wrong is not the problem — **being slow to accept you're wrong is**.
The fastest way to compound a loss is to delay the inevitable exit.

- Pros will often cut *before* their planned stop if they see the core reason for entry has been invalidated.

- This is not "fear" — this is tactical retreat.

Maintaining the Human Edge

Be careful:
If you try to become *too mechanical*, you risk killing the one thing a human trader has over an algorithm — contextual adaptability.

- The machine executes your plan without hesitation.

- The human adapts when the market shifts mid-trade.

The elite are **machine-like in discipline, human in adaptability**.
They don't freeze in the face of changing conditions, and they don't abandon their process on a whim.

The Execution Flow of a Professional Day Trader

1. **Morning** — Pre-load scenarios, size, and exact levels.

2. **During Session** — React only to pre-approved triggers.

3. **Post-Entry** — Manage risk first, profit second.

4. **Exit** — On invalidation or planned profit target.

5. **After Trade** — Quick notes on execution quality, not just trade outcome.

The Bottom Line

Execution is a skill you build, not a talent you're born with. If you can reduce hesitation, enforce loss acceptance, and manage trades like a surgeon, your edge will compound — not because your ideas are better, but because you extract maximum value from the ones you already have. The most brilliant analysis, the cleanest levels, the most advanced understanding of liquidity all collapse into nothing if your execution breaks down at the moment of decision.

At the professional level, the market does not reward the thinker, it rewards the operator. The sponsor cares nothing about your conviction or your theory — only whether you acted before the window closed. One second of hesitation turns a favorable entry into a chase. One act of defiance against your stop turns a controlled risk into career damage. One delayed exit takes a small scratch and multiplies it into a deep wound. Every error of execution has a magnifying effect, because the market is structured to extract maximum cost from hesitation and denial.

This is why institutions drill execution until it is reflexive. Decisions are pre-loaded before the bell: entry criteria, position size, exit conditions. Hotkeys are tested, brackets pre-armed, contingency plans rehearsed. In the moment of impact, there is no space for reflection, no room for debate, no negotiation with the tape. The action is instant, because survival depends on it. What amateurs call discipline, professionals treat as standard operating procedure.

Execution is not a detail to polish once you "have your strategy." Execution is the strategy. It is the last filter through which all preparation, analysis, and planning must pass — and it is the only filter that directly converts thought into P&L. You are not paid for ideas. You are not paid for effort. You are not even paid for being right. You are paid for the precision with which you translate your preparation into orders that hit the tape exactly where and when they should. If you truly want to compete at sponsor level, stop asking whether your ideas are good enough. Start asking whether your execution is clean enough. In the end, the market doesn't care who had the best thesis. It only records who got filled at the right price, who cut the loss before it metastasized, and who exited while others hesitated. The difference between the survivor and the casualty is never theory — it is always execution.

Chapter 23 — The Longevity Blueprint: Building a Career That Outlasts the Market Cycles

Day trading is seductive because of its speed.
You can turn ideas into capital in minutes. You can have a month's salary in an hour — or lose it in thirty seconds. But the **real game** is not about the thrill of one trade or one month.

It's about **staying in the arena long enough for your edge to become unstoppable**.

Longevity is the master key. Every great trader you've heard of — the ones still around decades later — survived market cycles, personal setbacks, regulatory changes, and the silent killer of all traders: **burnout**.

This chapter is your framework for not just making it, but **staying made**.

1. The Reality of Cycles

Markets move in cycles.
So does your performance.

- There will be months when everything you touch works. You'll feel invincible.

- There will be months when you can't seem to win a trade. You'll feel cursed.

The amateur treats these like random events. The professional understands they are **natural phases**. The job is to manage capital, mind, and energy across both — not blow up during the drawdown and not over-leverage during the hot streak.

2. Capital Preservation as a Career Skill

Your biggest competitive advantage isn't your next trade —
it's the fact that you're still around to take the next trade.

Longevity means:

- Trading smaller when you're cold to slow the
  drawdown.

- Trading larger when the market conditions match
  your edge, but without swinging into
  recklessness.

- Keeping a "never-break" rule on your capital
  floor — the amount you will never go below, no
  matter what.

3. The Energy Account

Most traders think only about their *cash* account. The pros
also track their **energy account**.

Trading drains mental bandwidth.
The more depleted you are, the more likely you are to:

- Overtrade.

- Miss obvious signals.

- Hesitate on A+ setups.

Pro tactics for energy preservation:

- **Scheduled days off** even during hot streaks.

- **Deliberate decompression** post-market to reset
  emotional state.

- **Strict sleep discipline** — tired traders are blind traders.

4. Continuous Edge Refinement

Your strategy today will not work forever. Markets evolve. Liquidity shifts. Algorithms adapt.

Longevity means you:

- Audit your edge quarterly — what's still working, what's decaying.

- Archive data to spot subtle changes in volatility, volume, and reaction to news.

- Test *adjacent* strategies without abandoning your core.

5. Avoiding Psychological Decay

The longer you trade, the more invisible your blind spots become.
Complacency kills — not instantly, but over years.

Signs of decay:

- You stop reviewing trades because "you already know what happened."

- You start believing you're immune to drawdowns.

- You take impulsive trades "for fun" because the account is big enough.

The cure is ruthless self-auditing — and occasionally **trading small again just to rebuild discipline**.

6. Building a Life Outside the Screen

Longevity is impossible if the market becomes your *only* identity.

- You'll over-attach to each outcome.

- You'll experience isolation that erodes decision quality.

Pros build other arenas of life where they win: fitness, relationships, creative outlets, travel.
These give you resilience when trading inevitably hits a cold patch.

7. Legacy Thinking

The ultimate sign of longevity is that your trading outlives your active participation.
This could mean:

- Building a fund or firm.

- Teaching others at a high level.

- Managing capital in a way that allows you to step back without losing wealth.

If your career ends the moment you stop staring at a Level 2 screen, you built a *job*, not a career.

Bottom Line

Surviving and thriving over decades is not luck — it is the result of enforceable systems. Longevity is built on four pillars: capital discipline, energy management, psychological resilience, and edge refinement. Each one has to be treated like risk management, because failure in any single pillar can erase years of progress.

Capital discipline means you never break your capital floor. If you decide that $100,000 is the base you will never touch, then no trade, no streak, and no excuse can dip you below it. This forces you to size down during cold periods and push size only when conditions align. Without a floor, every drawdown risks becoming terminal.

Energy management means treating your mental and physical state as a second account. Burnout is not a feeling — it is a form of drawdown that silently erodes decision quality. Professionals schedule recovery days, keep strict sleep discipline, and step back when fatigue clouds execution. They understand that a tired operator will overtrade, miss obvious signals, and hesitate when the edge finally appears.

Psychological resilience is the ability to face cycles without collapsing. Hot streaks and cold streaks are not random; they are inevitable. The amateur thinks a losing month means their system is broken, while the professional expects them and responds with smaller size, tighter focus, and patience until conditions turn. The trader who cannot endure cycles without emotional collapse will not survive long enough to benefit when their edge resurfaces.

Edge refinement means you never assume today's playbook will work forever. Markets evolve, liquidity shifts, and algorithms adapt. Longevity demands quarterly audits of what's working, archiving what's fading, and testing adjacent strategies. The pro who reviews, adjusts, and evolves will stay relevant. The one who coasts on what used to work eventually gets erased.

Longevity is not glamorous. It is not measured in screenshots of big wins or in one hot year. It is measured in the ability to keep trading year after year without a catastrophic break — to still be in the arena when most have been carried out. If you enforce capital floors, protect your energy, accept and manage cycles, and constantly refine your edge, you will not just trade for another month or year. You will be one of the few still operating decades later, when most of your competition has long disappeared. That endurance — not brilliance, not luck — is the real edge.

Chapter 24 — The Closing Playbook: Survival, Growth, and Domination

This is the distillation of everything.
It's not a pep talk, and it's not a recap.
It's the *operating system* you run as a professional day trader — every decision, every trade, every career phase filtered through these principles.

1. Survival Mode — Protect the Core

You do not get to growth or domination without survival. Survival means you stay in the game — financially, mentally, and physically.

Core Survival Laws:

- **Capital Floor:** Decide the absolute lowest your account will ever go and never breach it. If you hit it, you stop trading until you've rebuilt through other income or investments.

- **Trade Only A+ Conditions:** No setup, no trade. No "boredom trades." Every bad trade in survival mode is theft from your future self.

- **Tight Energy Management:** Fatigue is the silent killer. You have no business at the screens if you're not mentally sharp.

- **Ego Containment:** No revenge trading. No "I'll show the market." The market does not know you exist.

2. Growth Mode — Scale Without Dilution

Growth mode is where most traders blow it — they get bigger but sloppier.
Real growth is scaling *without losing the precision that got you here.*

Core Growth Laws:

- **Layer Size Gradually:** Never double your position size in one jump. Increase in controlled increments so execution quality doesn't suffer.

- **Keep the Old Playbook Alive:** As you explore new strategies, keep your core bread-and-butter setups in rotation.

- **Data is King:** You track every trade, every market condition, every emotional state. Patterns in your own behavior are as important as patterns in price.

- **Capital Allocation:** Assign capital to strategies by proven ROI, not by excitement. If 80% of your profits come from one setup, that setup gets the most capital.

3. Domination Mode — Control the Board

Domination mode is when you operate like the *sponsor* of the market, not just a participant. You understand positioning flows, liquidity games, and the mechanics of mass psychology. You are no longer reactive — you are engineering outcomes.

To "engineer outcomes" you must think like inventory, not like opinion. Sponsors dictate the auction by manipulating **where** retail must commit, **when** they must liquidate, and **how** flows intersect with the calendar. In Domination mode:

- **Liquidity Awareness:** Before each session, pre-map **three traps** where retail must puke. This means identifying (1) stop clusters above/below prior H/L, (2) LVN corridors where price accelerates on crumbs, (3) strike walls where dealers must hedge. Your executions are not random—they're designed to *harvest* these pools.

- **Time Mastery:** You know the rhythms of your market's day — the open, midday lull, power hour — and you play each with a tailored plan.

- **Macro-to-Micro Link:** Domination isn't just intraday tape—it's aligning your trades with structural currents/macro backdrops and using it to choose which instruments to attack. If rates fall and gamma is short, you expect explosive upside. If CTAs are deleveraging, you expect air pockets. Every micro play sits inside a macro frame.

- **Invisible Hand Execution:** In Domination, you understand you can create your own liquidity. You stagger orders across venues, use icebergs to bait fills, by strategically sizing, pacing, and timing your entries so you never move the market against yourself. Retail waits for signals; you *design* them.

Domination is not about being right—it's about controlling the flows so others are forced to be wrong.

4. The Three-Mode Integration

Survival. Growth. Domination. They are not separate stages — they are gears. In a hot streak, you may shift from Growth to Domination in a week. In a drawdown, you may slam back into Survival in one day. The key is to shift gears without hesitation or ego.

Think of the modes as a **transmission system.** Survival is first gear—you move slow but you can't stall. Growth is second gear—speed increases as long as traction holds. Domination is third gear—maximum torque, but dangerous if the road slips. Integration means knowing **when to change gears**:

- **Up-Shift Triggers:** Expectancy ≥ + 0.40R over 20 trades, adherence ≥ 90%, volatility clean. That's your clearance to move from Growth → Domination.

- **Down-Shift Triggers:** Two rule breaches, SRU breach, or Energy ≤ 3 triggers an instant step back. Domination → Growth or Growth → Survival is not failure—it's transmission protection.

- **Gear Discipline:** Never trade Domination rules in Survival context. For example: if you're in a drawdown, you cut size immediately instead of "earning it back." Integration means ego never overrides the mode.

The operator's edge is not just system—it's *adaptive system*. Integration is the ability to shift gears mid-battle without hesitation.

5. The Self-Override Protocol

Every trader needs an emergency switch — a way to stop themselves before they burn everything down.

The 3-Step Override:

1. **Pause Execution** — Stop trading immediately if you feel tilt, frustration, or overconfidence.

2. **Step Out** — Leave the desk physically. Breathe. Eat. Walk. Lift. Anything but trading.

3. **Re-Enter Only With Criteria** — You cannot return unless you have a pre-written setup that matches your playbook 100%.

6. The 20-Year View

If you plan like you'll be trading for 20+ years:
You won't swing for the fences every day.
You'll value capital preservation as much as capital growth.
You'll build a body and mind that can withstand decades of screen time.
You'll create income streams around trading so you're never forced into bad trades to pay bills.

Longevity is the ultimate edge. Anyone can get hot for a quarter. Only the professional builds systems to still be in the game 20 years later.

- **Edge Renewal:** Every 3–6 months, retire one decayed setup and pilot one new one at minimal size. Never let your playbook ossify—markets evolve, your edge must evolve with them.

- **Capital Rings:** Maintain three rings of capital: *Preservation* (never touched), *Operational* (daily deployment), *Expansion* (profits recycled into tech, data, or outside assets). This ensures no single market shock erases your future.

- **Redundancy:** Second ISP, UPS power, backup broker, written phone-order scripts. Professionals plan for failure before it happens.

- **Legacy Mindset:** Wealth is not just P&L—it's freedom and continuity. Document your playbook, your case files, your risk rules. Your career is an asset; treat it as something that can be handed down.

Body Protocols (Physical Resilience)

• **Vision Health:** Annual eye exams, blue-light filtering lenses, screen brightness calibrated to ambient light, and strict breaks every 50–60 minutes (20–20–20 rule: look 20 feet away for 20 seconds every 20 minutes).

• **Ergonomics:** Adjustable chair with lumbar support, desk height matched to elbow level, monitor tops at eye level. This prevents spinal wear and repetitive strain.

• **Movement:** At least 2–3 short workouts daily: standing desk rotation, resistance band pulls, squats/pushups between sessions. Cardiovascular training 3–4x/week to maintain circulation and focus.

• **Nutrition:** High-protein, low-glycemic meals; no heavy sugar spikes during trading hours. Hydration target: 3–4 liters/day. Limit caffeine past noon to preserve sleep cycles.

Mind Protocols (Cognitive Resilience)

• **Sleep Discipline:** 7–8 hours minimum, ideally consistent bedtime/wake cycle. Cognitive sharpness degrades exponentially under chronic sleep debt.

• **Mental Reset Blocks:** 2–3 breaks away from screens during the session, plus one longer decompression block post-market (walk, lift, meditation).

- **Stress Containment:** Breath work (box breathing 4-4-4-4), journaling micro-triggers, and a hard "shutoff" routine after the bell so trading stress doesn't bleed into life.

- **Skill Cross-Training:** Reading outside markets (math, history, psychology), strategy games, or chess. Keeps neuroplasticity high and decision-making flexible.

Systemization

Treat body/mind like you treat capital:

- Log **sleep hours, energy score, exercise done** → review weekly just like you review trades.

- Build a "**health dashboard**" parallel to your trading dashboard. If energy <3, if sleep <6.5h, if HRV (heart rate variability) is down, you cut size.

The 20-year view reframes every choice: *Am I protecting the operator I'll be in ten years?* If the answer is no, you're already dying.

7. Closing Mandate

You do not rise to the market.
You fall to the level of your preparation and discipline.
This book has given you the structural edge, the psychological armor, and the operational framework.

Now your only job is to **run it without compromise**.

Chapter 25 — The Trader's Oath: Building a Life Worthy of the Game

You are here because you chose one of the most unforgiving games ever created.
This is not poker, not sports, not entrepreneurship in the traditional sense.
In trading, the market can take from you **instantly**, and it doesn't care about your degree, your résumé, or how badly you "want it."

But that's what makes it worth it.

The market is **the mirror**.
It reflects you — every fear, every hesitation, every fantasy of success, every blind spot you've refused to face.
And every day, you get to step into that mirror and decide:
Do I come back stronger, sharper, and more in control than I was yesterday?
Or do I keep letting this thing own me?

1. The Truth About Why You're Failing

Let's strip away the excuses.

- It's not the market makers.

- It's not the algorithms.

- It's not because "the market is manipulated."

You're failing because you've refused to operate at the standard this game demands.
You've been letting emotions call the shots.
You've been trading without a razor-sharp playbook.
You've been acting like this is a side hustle, not a professional operation. And here's the truth: the market punishes *pretenders*.

2. The Switch

There is a moment every elite trader has — where they flip the switch.
This is when they decide:

"I will no longer trade like an amateur. I will become the sponsor of my own operation."

That switch means:

- You cut every distraction.

- You remove every toxic influence that pulls your focus from the game.

- You track every trade, every thought, every execution — because you refuse to lie to yourself anymore.

- You start managing yourself like a fund manager, not a retail hobbyist.

And the day you flip that switch, you are **no longer competing with random retail traders** — you are now training to compete with people who have billions behind them and decades in the game.

3. The Long War

If you think this is a one-year grind to "make it," you're already dead in the water.
The best traders think in **decades**.
They build wealth in layers — first survival, then growth, then domination.
They know there will be years where they crush it and

years where they barely break even — but they never, ever blow themselves up.

The amateurs want fireworks.
The professionals want **compound growth**.

4. The Real Wealth

You think wealth is the money? That's just the scoreboard.
The real wealth is **freedom** — the ability to live on your own terms.
To never answer to a boss again.
To work a 90-minute day and make more than someone else makes in a month.
To walk away from toxic people, environments, and obligations without fear.

That's why you're here.
And the only thing standing between you and that life is your own discipline.

5. The Trader's Oath

Before you take another trade, you make this oath — to yourself, not to me:

I will protect my capital as I would my own life, because it is my life in this game.
I will execute only when my edge is present and proven.
I will never let one day, one trade, or one streak define me.
I will operate like a professional in every aspect of my career.
I will constantly refine myself — mentally, emotionally, and technically — until the market itself respects me.
I will not quit until I have built the freedom and life I came here for.

6. Your New Baseline

From here on out, "good enough" is gone.
The new baseline is precision, professionalism, and constant iteration.
You don't have to be perfect — but you have to be better every single week.

The market is not the enemy.
The market is the ultimate training ground.
It will pay you beyond your imagination — but only after it's broken every bad habit you have and rebuilt you from the ground up.

If you follow this playbook, that process won't take decades.
It will take as long as it takes for you to stop lying to yourself and start running your life like a trader who actually deserves to win.

When this book closes, the game begins.
The screens are waiting.
The opportunity is waiting.
But the market does not wait for hesitation.

Decide right now:
Do you step into this with everything you have?
Or do you keep pretending you'll get serious "someday"?

There is no someday.
There is only today.
And today — you either flip the switch, or you get left behind.

Appendix — Operator's Lexicon

Absorption — Large passive orders soak up aggressive flow at a price, stalling movement without reversal; a sponsor footprint.

ADR (Average Daily Range) — Typical session range; sets realistic targets and stop width.

Aggression Layer — Highest-risk tranche of capital; deployed only when environment, timing, and setup are fully aligned.

Autopsy Oath — Your standing pledge to avoid the seven lethal errors; survival discipline in one page.

Auction Imbalance (MOO/MOC) — Net buy/sell interest queued for the open/close; often dictates the final push.

BBO (Best Bid/Offer) — National inside quote; baseline for fill quality and midpoint logic.

Benchmarking Pressure — Urgency when funds must mark to VWAP/close; explains 3:30–4:00 squeezes.

Book Reload — Reappearance of size at the same price after a print; classic absorption tell.

Breakout Trap — Engineered push through a level to trigger stops and reverse into fresh liquidity.

Broker Internalization — Orders matched against captive flow; changes your read of "what hit the exchange."

Calendar Gravity — Pull of scheduled flows: OpEx, rebalances, month/quarter-end, Fed, earnings windows.

Call Wall / Put Floor — High-OI strikes that cap/prop price via dealer hedging.

Capital Floor — Account level you will never breach; hit it and you stop trading until rebuilt.

Closing Auction (MOC/LOC) — Primary print for benchmarkers; where desks finalize marks.

Corporate Buybacks (10b5-1) — Programmatic bid that supports tape during non-blackout windows.

CTA Flow — Vol-targeting/trend systems that lever up in calm and delever in stress.

Dark Pool / ATS — Off-exchange venue for size; explains lit "fails" after the real trade already crossed.

Decision Stack — Pre-loaded if/then playbook that removes hesitation in live action.

Delta Hedging — Dealer spot adjustment to offset option exposure; creates reflexive moves.

Demand Zone — Area built by sustained absorption; future launchpad on retests.

Depth of Book — Queued liquidity beyond top of book; useful for gauging real capacity.

Discretionary Peg — Resting order with a small auto-reach; captures flow without chasing.

Ego Override — Refusal to cut when wrong; source code of blow-ups.

Execution Algo (TWAP/VWAP/POV) — Slicers used to mask size; trackable footprints.

Execution Environment — Physical/digital/mental cockpit that minimizes latency and decision drag.

Exhaustion — Aggressive flow stops printing and price stalls; often precedes reversal.

Failure Autopsy — Brutal post-mortem that tags the real cause (size, tilt, phase, calendar, narrative, activity, ego).

Fill Quality — Slippage versus mid/VWAP/benchmark; hard metric of execution.

Flip Zone (Gamma/Delta) — Level where dealer hedging behavior flips; volatility behavior changes.

Footprint (Order-Flow Imprint) — Print clusters that show net aggressive pressure at price.

Gamma Flip — Strike/region where dealers switch from vol suppression (long γ) to amplification (short γ).

Gap Fill — Return into prior session gap; often a liquidity harvest, not "fair value."

Grind Day — Low-vol directional day often driven by CTA participation.

Hide-Not-Slide — Hidden order type that stays concealed through price moves; mitigates signaling.

High-Volume Node (HVN) — Price region of heavy prior trade; acts like a magnet.

Iceberg (Reserve) Order — Shows small, hides large; used to stealth-accumulate/distribute.

Imbalance Feed — Live MOO/MOC data; roadmap for power-close behavior.

Internalization — Wholesaler fills against captive flow; lit tape lags true interest.

Journal Hit-Rate (Flow Read) — % of sessions your sponsor/phase read was correct; leading indicator of edge health.

Kill Shot — Rare A+ setup with full alignment; deploy max allowable risk.

Kill Switch — Hard stop on session/week loss or behavior breach; triggers flatten and shutdown.

Latency — Decision-to-print delay; key driver of slippage and miss risk.

Liquidity Hunt — Raid into stop clusters to source fills; can be continuation or reversal.

Liquidity Vacuum (LVN) — Thin pocket between volume nodes; price accelerates on crumbs.

Long Gamma — Dealer regime damping volatility; fades pushes back toward strikes.

Low-Volume Node (LVN) — See Liquidity Vacuum.

Mental Auto-Scaling — Automatic size cut when stability slips; preserves capital and state.

Midpoint Peg — Executes at NBBO mid; stealthy for accumulation/distribution.

Microstructure — Mechanics of how orders become prints; your execution physics.

Monthly Risk Budget (MRB) — Pre-allocated loss ammo for the month; stops death by a thousand cuts.

MOO/LOC/MOC — Market-on-Open/Limit-on-Close/Market-on-Close instructions for auctions.

Mode Stack — Surveillance → Probe → Campaign → Extract; institutional execution cycle.

Narrative Machine — Media/PR flow that justifies moves after sponsors acted; smoke, not thrust.

NBBO — National Best Bid/Offer; basis for mid and order protection.

Net Delta — Aggregate directional exposure from options/stock; frames dealer pressure.

Operator's Oath — Daily contract: trade sponsorship, respect the clock, protect capital.

OpEx Pin Risk — Price hugging big strikes into expiration due to hedging flow.

Order Protection (Reg NMS) — Routing rule that enforces NBBO; affects mid/pegged fills.

POV (Participation) Algo — Slices at a target % of market volume.

Phase of the Day — Overnight, pre-market, open trap, midday drift, power hour; each with distinct tactics.

Pin Risk — Exposure around a strike where option exercise/assignment is uncertain.

Price Discovery vs. Liquidity Transfer — Retail myth versus reality; the tape serves inventory transfer.

Rebalance Flow — Calendar weight changes that force end-day/quarter prints.

Reclaim — Fast retake of VWAP/PDH/PDL after a stop run; strong sponsorship tell.

Reserve Order — See Iceberg; hides real size while quoting a stub.

Risk Budget — Pre-defined loss tolerance across trade/ session/month; enforces survivability.

Routing (Directed/Smart) — Venue selection strategy; lit for signaling, dark for stealth.

Scalability Ladder — Planned, incremental size increases tied to data, not emotion.

Session Risk Unit (SRU) — Max session loss (e.g., 2–3× TRU) that triggers stop-trading.

Short Gamma — Dealer regime amplifying volatility; chases moves away from strikes.

Slippage — Unpaid tax from latency and routing; keep a ledger.

Sponsor — Participant with mandate and flow sufficient to bend the tape.

Stop-Run — Intentional sweep to trigger stops and unlock liquidity.

Supply Zone — Area built by distribution; future ceiling on retests.

Tape (Time & Sales) — Raw prints; earliest, least-interpreted signal of intent.

Tilt Loop — Revenge sequence after a loss; ends careers if unbroken.

Time-at-Price (TPO/Profile) — Distribution of trade by price/time; maps value and vacuums.

Trade Risk Unit (TRU) — Fixed % risk per trade (0.5–1% typical pro standard).

Trend Day / Range Day — Day types that dictate expectation management, entries, and exits.

TWAP (Time-Weighted Average Price) — Schedule-based slicer; flattens footprint.

VWAP (Volume-Weighted Average Price) — Institutional benchmark and intraday gravity center.

Unwind — Sponsor exits inventory into strength/weakness with minimal footprint.

Vacuum Walk — Deliberate drive through an LVN to accelerate repricing.

Vol Targeting — Systematic scaling with realized vol; CTA hallmark.

War Room — Your console, rules, and protocols; the operating theater.

Window Dressing — End-period prints to improve optics versus benchmarks.

Zone Engineering — Manufacturing a base/ceiling to bait participation, then abandoning it.

www.ingramcontent.com/pod-product-compliance
Lightning Source LLC
Chambersburg PA
CBHW061312220326
41599CB00026B/4849